AF700246

Secrets of Roth Conversion Strategies For Retirees

USING FIXED INDEXED ANNUITIES

By Jeff Weidner
Boom Retirement Solutions

Published by Boom Retirement Solutions
Wake Forest, NC

Limited Liability and Disclaimer of Warranty:
Every effort has been made by the author and publisher to ensure the accuracy and completeness of this book. However, the publisher and author make no representations or warranties of any kind, express or implied, about the accuracy or completeness of the contents. They specifically disclaim all implied warranties of merchantability or fitness for a particular purpose.
The strategies and advice in this book may not be suitable for every situation. Neither the author nor the publisher shall be held liable for any loss of profit or other damages, including but not limited to special, incidental, consequential, or other damages arising out of the use or misuse of the information provided. Readers should consult with a qualified professional for personalized guidance.

First Edition
Published in Wake Forest, NC by Boom Retirement Solutions, 2025

Summary:
This guide provides the secrets to performing partial Roth conversions using Fixed Indexed Annuities every retiree should know to reduce tax liabilities, minimize Required Minimum Distributions (RMDs), and achieve lasting financial success in retirement.

Author: Jeff Weidner

Dedication

To all those approaching retirement, may you find the confidence and clarity to make the most of your retirement assets, reduce your taxes and create the retirement you deserve.

And to my family, whose support made this book possible.

Download your Free Book

https://books.jeffweidner.com/free

SCAN ME

DOWNLOAD FREE BOOK

Acknowledgments

Writing a book about Secret Roth Conversion Strategies for Retirees that is both comprehensive and accessible requires the support and expertise of many individuals. I would like to express my deepest gratitude to:

My clients, whose questions and concerns helped shape the content of this book. Your trust in me to guide you through retirement planning decisions has been both a privilege and an inspiration.

The team at Boom Retirement Solutions, whose dedication to serving our clients with excellence provides the foundation for everything we do. Your commitment to helping people create secure retirement income strategies makes our work meaningful and impactful.

My mentors in the financial services industry taught me the importance of putting clients first and always continuing to learn. Your guidance has been invaluable in developing the expertise shared in these pages.

The editorial team, whose careful attention to detail helped ensure this complex subject matter is presented clearly and accurately. Your contributions have made this book more accessible and useful for readers.

My family, whose patience and support during the writing process made this book possible. Your encouragement kept me going through long hours of research and writing. Finally, to you, the reader, for taking this important step toward understanding and minimizing your tax liabilities in retirement. Your commitment to creating a secure retirement future is admirable.

How to Use This Book for Roth Conversions

This book is designed to serve as a comprehensive guide for retirees and pre-retirees considering Roth conversions as part of their financial strategy. Whether you're just starting to explore the concept or are ready to take actionable steps, this book provides a step-by-step roadmap to help you achieve a tax-free retirement. Here's how to get the most out of this resource:

1. Understand the Basics

Start with the foundational chapters to learn what a Roth conversion is and why it might be beneficial for your retirement strategy.

Familiarize yourself with key terms, such as tax-deferred accounts, Roth IRAs, Required Minimum Distributions (RMDs), and Fixed Indexed Annuities (FIAs). The Glossary of Terms at the end of the book is a great reference for unfamiliar concepts.

2. Assess Your Current Situation

Use the evaluation tools and checklists provided in the book to take a snapshot of your financial situation. This includes:

Reviewing your current tax bracket.

Calculating the total value of your traditional IRA or 401(k).

Identifying your financial goals for retirement.

This initial step will help you determine whether a Roth conversion is right for you and how much you might consider converting.

3. Learn the Strategies

Dive into the strategy chapters to discover how Roth conversions can reduce future taxes, eliminate RMDs, and leave a tax-free inheritance for your beneficiaries.

Explore specific tactics, such as phased conversions, using FIAs to manage conversion taxes, and timing strategies to stay within favorable tax brackets.

4. Create Your Action Plan

Use the step-by-step implementation guide to structure your Roth conversion process. This includes:

Determining the optimal amount to convert.

Timing conversions during low-income years or market downturns.

Preparing for the tax bill associated with the conversion.

Learn how to avoid common pitfalls, such as triggering higher Medicare premiums or Social Security taxation.

5. Tailor the Strategy to Your Needs

If you have more complex financial needs, refer to the advanced strategies section for insights on using multiple FIAs, leveraging income riders, and incorporating Roth conversions into estate planning or charitable giving.

6. Monitor and Adjust

Retirement planning is not a one-time event. The ongoing management chapter provides guidance on how to:

Review your strategy annually.

Adjust for changes in tax laws, personal circumstances, or market conditions.

Ensure your plan continues to align with your long-term financial goals.

7. Seek Professional Guidance

While this book equips you with the knowledge to make informed decisions, consulting with a qualified financial advisor or tax professional is highly recommended. They can help you navigate complex rules and tailor strategies to your unique situation.

8. Take Action

The information in this book is most valuable when applied. Use the case studies, real-world examples, and practical tips to confidently take steps toward a secure, tax-free retirement.

By following the guidance in this book, you'll gain the clarity and confidence needed to make Roth conversions a key part of your financial strategy. Whether your goal is to reduce taxes, preserve your wealth, or create a legacy for your loved ones, this book will serve as your trusted roadmap.

We specialize in Roth Conversions using Fixed Indexed Annuities. If you need help or guidance, feel free to book a call using the QR code below..

SCAN TO SCHEDULE

AN APPOINTMENT

Table of Contents

Introduction

Retirement is one of the most significant milestones in life—a time to finally enjoy the freedom you've worked so hard to achieve. Yet, for many, the transition comes with a nagging question: *Will my money last as long as I do?* This uncertainty, compounded by rising taxes, market volatility, and healthcare costs, can leave retirees and soon-to-be retirees feeling overwhelmed.

That's where this book comes in.

At its core, this guide is about empowering you with the knowledge and strategies to secure a financially stable and tax-efficient retirement. By combining two powerful tools—Roth conversions and Fixed Indexed Annuities (FIAs)—you can protect your assets from future tax hikes, market downturns, and unnecessary financial stress. But this isn't just a book about products or policies. It's about a strategy that ensures your retirement savings work *for* you, not against you.

Why Roth Conversions Matter

You've likely heard the term "Roth conversion," but what does it really mean? At a high level, a Roth conversion allows you to move money from a tax-deferred account, like a traditional IRA or 401(k), into a Roth IRA, where it can grow tax-free for life. However, this decision isn't one-size-fits-all. It requires careful planning to weigh the short-term tax cost against long-term benefits like eliminating Required Minimum Distributions (RMDs) and leaving a tax-free legacy for your loved ones.

This book will walk you through the nuances of Roth conversions, addressing common misconceptions—like the fear of paying too much in taxes upfront—and showing you how to use these conversions to your advantage.

Enter Fixed Indexed Annuities

While Roth conversions offer incredible tax advantages, the process of funding them often raises a key question: *How do I pay the taxes without jeopardizing my retirement lifestyle?* That's where Fixed Indexed Annuities come in.

FIAs are a unique retirement tool that combines growth potential with protection from market losses. With features like income riders and index-linked returns, they provide a steady stream of income that can be used to pay conversion taxes while keeping your core retirement assets intact. This combination not only simplifies the conversion process but also adds another layer of financial security to your retirement plan.

What You'll Learn

This book is divided into four parts to guide you step-by-step:

- **Part I: Foundation Concepts**
  Before diving into strategies, you'll gain a clear understanding of Roth conversions and Fixed Indexed Annuities. We'll break down the benefits, potential pitfalls, and key considerations, ensuring you have a solid foundation.

- **Part II: The Strategy**
  Here, we'll explore how Roth conversions and FIAs can work together seamlessly. You'll learn how to structure this strategy to minimize taxes, maximize income, and achieve long-term financial stability.

- **Part III: Implementation**
  Knowing the strategy is one thing; implementing it is another. This section provides a step-by-step guide to evaluating your situation, choosing the right FIA, and avoiding common mistakes during the conversion process.

- **Part IV: Ongoing Management**
  Retirement planning isn't a one-and-done process. In this final section, we'll cover how to monitor, adjust, and fine-tune your strategy over time to ensure it continues to meet your evolving needs.

A Practical, Actionable Approach

This book isn't filled with fluff or abstract theories. Instead, it's a practical, actionable guide designed for retirees and soon-to-be retirees who want clarity and control over their financial future. With hypothetical case studies and easy-to-follow explanations, you'll see exactly how these strategies can work in real life.

Whether you're concerned about rising taxes, outliving your money, or protecting your assets for the next generation, the tools and insights in this book are here to help.

Your financial future is in your hands, and with the right knowledge and strategies, it can be brighter than you ever imagined. Let's get started.

Chapter 1: Understanding Roth Conversions

What is a Roth Conversion?

At its core, a Roth conversion is a financial strategy that allows you to move money from a tax-deferred retirement account—such as a traditional IRA or 401(k)—into a Roth IRA. When you execute this conversion, you'll pay taxes on the amount moved in the year of the conversion. However, the money in the Roth IRA then grows tax-free, and qualified withdrawals during retirement are also tax-free. This fundamental shift from "tax-deferred" to "tax-free" is what makes Roth conversions so appealing.

To understand the mechanics of a Roth conversion, it's helpful to think of it as prepaying your taxes. With traditional retirement accounts, you receive an upfront tax benefit by deferring taxes on your contributions and investment growth until you withdraw the funds in retirement. However, these withdrawals are subject to ordinary income tax at whatever rate applies to you at the time. A Roth IRA flips this model on its head: you pay taxes upfront, but all future growth and withdrawals are entirely tax-free as long as you meet the account's requirements.

The process itself is relatively straightforward. You instruct your financial institution to transfer funds from your traditional IRA or 401(k) into a Roth IRA. This can be done as a direct transfer, where the funds move directly between accounts, or as a 60-day rollover, where you temporarily hold the funds before depositing them into the Roth IRA. Direct transfers are generally recommended to avoid potential tax complications.

It's important to note that not all retirement accounts are eligible for Roth conversions. For example, some employer-sponsored 401(k) plans may not allow in-plan conversions to a Roth 401(k). In such cases, you would need to roll over the 401(k) to a traditional IRA first and then execute the Roth conversion. Additionally, while there are no income limits for performing a Roth conversion, the amount you convert will be added to your taxable income for the year, which can impact your tax bracket and eligibility for certain tax credits or deductions. In essence, a Roth conversion is a strategic move that requires careful planning and consideration of your current and future financial situation. It's not a decision to be made lightly, but for many retirees and pre-retirees, it can be a powerful tool to secure long-term financial stability.

Benefits and Drawbacks of Roth Conversions

Benefits of Roth Conversions

1. **Tax-Free Growth and Withdrawals** One of the most compelling benefits of a Roth conversion is the opportunity for tax-free growth. Once your money is in a Roth IRA, all investment gains are shielded from taxes. Additionally, when you withdraw the funds during retirement, the withdrawals are entirely tax-free as long as you

meet the account's requirements. This provides peace of mind, as you'll no longer have to worry about future tax hikes affecting your retirement income.

2. **Avoiding Required Minimum Distributions (RMDs)** Traditional IRAs and 401(k)s require you to start taking RMDs at age 73, whether you need the money or not. These mandatory withdrawals are taxed as ordinary income and can push you into a higher tax bracket. Roth IRAs, however, are not subject to RMDs, giving you greater control over your retirement income and allowing your money to continue growing tax-free for as long as you want.

3. **Reducing Future Tax Burden** By converting to a Roth IRA, you pay taxes on the converted amount at today's rates, which may be lower than future rates. This is particularly advantageous if you expect tax rates to increase due to changes in tax laws or if you anticipate being in a higher tax bracket during retirement. Additionally, reducing your taxable income in retirement can help minimize taxes on Social Security benefits and Medicare premiums.

4. **Tax-Free Inheritance for Beneficiaries** A Roth IRA can be an excellent tool for estate planning. Unlike traditional IRAs, which require beneficiaries to pay taxes on inherited funds, Roth IRAs allow your heirs to receive distributions tax-free. This can significantly reduce the financial

burden on your loved ones and preserve more of your hard-earned savings for future generations.

5. **Flexibility in Retirement Planning** Roth IRAs provide unmatched flexibility. Because withdrawals are not taxed, you can better manage your income streams in retirement. This flexibility can be particularly useful when facing unexpected expenses, market downturns, or changes in your financial situation. It also allows you to optimize your retirement income by strategically withdrawing from different accounts to minimize overall taxes.

Drawbacks of Roth Conversions

1. **Upfront Tax Cost** The most significant drawback of a Roth conversion is the upfront tax bill. When you convert funds, the amount transferred is treated as taxable income in the year of the conversion. This can push you into a higher tax bracket and may result in a larger-than-expected tax liability. For this reason, careful planning is essential to avoid unnecessary financial strain.

2. **Potential Impact on Medicare Premiums and Social Security** Because the converted amount is added to your taxable income, it can increase your Modified Adjusted Gross Income (MAGI). A higher MAGI can lead to increased Medicare premiums (IRMAA) and taxes on your Social Security benefits. These impacts need to be factored into your overall strategy to ensure the conversion is beneficial in the long run.

3. **Market Volatility Risk** If the market takes a downturn shortly after you convert, the value of your converted assets may decline, making it feel like you've paid taxes on "lost" money. While this can be frustrating, the long-term benefits of tax-free growth often outweigh short-term fluctuations. Additionally, converting during a market dip can be advantageous, as you'll pay taxes on a lower account value. This is another great reason to use a fixed indexed annuity to perform your partial Roth conversions. Fixed Indexed Annuities can't lose money due to market downturns or volatility. We will get into more details about this later in the book.

4. **Timing and Execution Challenges** The timing of a Roth conversion is critical. Converting too much in a single year can push you into a higher tax bracket, while converting too little may not maximize the long-term benefits. Additionally, the process requires precise execution, including understanding IRS rules and completing the necessary paperwork. Mistakes can lead to penalties or missed opportunities.

5. **Uncertainty About Future Tax Policies** While the current tax laws favor Roth conversions for many individuals, future changes in tax policy could impact their effectiveness. For example, if tax rates are reduced or if new regulations affect Roth accounts, the benefits of a conversion may not be as significant as initially anticipated. However, many experts agree that the potential for rising tax rates makes Roth conversions a prudent

choice in most cases. When the TCJA (Tax Cut and Jobs Act) tax cuts expire at the end of 2025 most income brackets will increase 3-5%. This is obviously subject to change but taxes rarely go down and stay down for very long.

Balancing the Benefits and Drawbacks

A Roth conversion is not a one-size-fits-all strategy. It requires a comprehensive analysis of your financial situation, including your current and future tax brackets, income needs, and estate planning goals. For many individuals, the long-term benefits outweigh the short-term costs, especially when combined with strategies like using Fixed Indexed Annuities to manage conversion taxes. However, it's essential to work with a knowledgeable financial advisor to determine whether a Roth conversion is right for you and to develop a personalized plan that aligns with your goals.

In the next section, we'll explore who should consider Roth conversions, some of the IRS rules and guidelines. And common Roth conversion mistakes.

Who Should Consider a Roth Conversion?

Roth conversions are not a universal solution, but they can be highly advantageous for certain individuals. Below are some scenarios where a Roth conversion may be particularly beneficial:

1. **Those Expecting Higher Future Tax Rates** If you believe tax rates will increase in the future—either due to changes in legislation or your personal financial situation—a Roth conversion can help lock in today's lower tax rates. This is especially relevant for younger retirees who are currently in a lower tax bracket than they expect to be later in life.

2. **Retirees in a Tax Bracket Gap** Many retirees experience a gap between their working years and the time when they must start taking RMDs or claiming Social Security benefits. This gap often places them in a lower tax bracket, making it an ideal time to perform Roth conversions without incurring excessive taxes.

3. **High-Net-Worth Individuals** For those with significant assets, Roth conversions can reduce the size of taxable estates and provide a tax-free inheritance for beneficiaries. High-net-worth individuals often use Roth IRAs as part of their estate planning strategy to minimize the tax burden on heirs.

4. **Those Concerned About RMDs** If you don't want to be forced into taking RMDs from a traditional IRA, converting to a Roth IRA eliminates this requirement. This can be particularly advantageous if you don't need the income and prefer to let your investments grow tax-free.

5. **Individuals Seeking Tax Diversification** Diversifying your retirement accounts between tax-deferred, tax-free, and taxable options can provide greater flexibility and control over your income in retirement. A Roth IRA adds a valuable tax-free component to this mix, making it easier to manage your overall tax liability.

6. **Younger Investors with Long Time Horizons** The longer your money has to grow, the more you

can benefit from the tax-free growth of a Roth IRA. Younger investors or early retirees with decades of potential growth ahead are ideal candidates for Roth conversions.

7. **Charitably Inclined Individuals** Roth conversions can complement charitable giving strategies. For example, by converting assets to a Roth IRA, you can free up other taxable accounts to fund charitable contributions, potentially maximizing the tax benefits of your philanthropy.

Key IRS Rules and Guidelines

When performing a Roth conversion, understanding the IRS rules is essential to avoid penalties and ensure compliance. Here are the most critical guidelines to keep in mind:

1. **No Income Limits for Conversions** Unlike Roth IRA <u>contributions</u>, which have income limits, there are no income restrictions for Roth <u>conversions</u>. Anyone, regardless of income level, can convert their traditional IRA or 401(k) to a Roth IRA.

2. **Taxable Amounts** The amount you convert is treated as taxable income for the year of the conversion. This means you'll need to plan for the additional tax liability, which can increase your tax bracket. Refer to IRS Publication 590-B for detailed guidelines on calculating the taxable amount.

3. **No Contribution Limits for Conversions** Unlike contributions to a Roth IRA, which are capped at $6,500 annually (or $7,500 if you're 50 or older in 2024), there are no limits on the amount you can

convert in a single year. However, converting too much can push you into a higher tax bracket, so careful planning is essential.

4. **Five-Year Rule** The five-year rule applies to Roth conversions. Each converted amount must remain in the Roth IRA for at least five years before it can be withdrawn without penalties. This rule ensures that the account is used for long-term retirement savings rather than short-term tax benefits.

5. **Timing Considerations** Conversions must be completed by December 31 of the calendar year to count for that year's taxes. Unlike IRA contributions, which can be made up until the tax filing deadline, conversions have a stricter timeline. Consult IRS Publication 590-A for more details.

6. **Pro-Rata Rule** If you have both pre-tax and after-tax funds in your traditional IRA, the IRS requires you to calculate the taxable portion of your conversion using the pro-rata rule. This rule can complicate conversions, so it's essential to work with a tax advisor to ensure accurate calculations.

7. **Backdoor Roth IRAs** High-income earners who don't qualify for direct Roth IRA contributions often use the backdoor Roth IRA strategy. This involves contributing to a traditional IRA and then converting those funds to a Roth IRA. While effective, this strategy must comply with the pro-rata rule to avoid unexpected tax consequences.

Common Roth Conversion Mistakes

1. **Failing to Plan for the Tax Bill** One of the most common mistakes is underestimating the tax liability of a Roth conversion. Without proper planning, the additional taxable income can push you into a higher tax bracket, increase your Medicare premiums, or trigger taxes on Social Security benefits.

2. **Converting Too Much at Once** While it may be tempting to convert a large amount in a single year, this can result in a hefty tax bill. A multi-year conversion strategy is often more effective, allowing you to spread the tax burden over several years and stay within a lower tax bracket.

3. **Ignoring the Five-Year Rule** Some investors overlook the five-year rule, only to face penalties when withdrawing converted funds. Understanding the timeline for penalty-free withdrawals is essential to avoid unexpected costs.

4. **Not Accounting for State Taxes** Many people forget to consider state income taxes when planning a Roth conversion. Depending on your state's tax laws, the conversion could result in a significant additional tax liability.

5. **Overlooking Medicare Premiums (IRMAA)** A Roth conversion can increase your MAGI, leading to higher Medicare premiums. Failing to account for this impact can result in unpleasant surprises down the line.

6. **Not Working with a Professional** Roth conversions involve complex rules and calculations. Working with a financial advisor or tax professional can help you avoid costly mistakes and ensure that your conversion strategy aligns with your long-term goals.

By understanding who should consider a Roth conversion, adhering to IRS rules, and avoiding common pitfalls, you can make informed decisions that maximize the benefits of this powerful financial strategy. In the next chapter, we'll explore how Fixed Indexed Annuities can complement your Roth conversion strategy, providing additional security and tax advantages.

Chapter 2: Fixed Indexed Annuities Explained

What is a Fixed Indexed Annuity?

A Fixed Indexed Annuity (FIA) is a financial product designed to provide both growth potential and protection for your retirement savings. It's a type of annuity that offers the opportunity to earn interest based on the performance of a market index, like the S&P 500, while ensuring that your principal is protected from market losses. This combination of growth and security makes FIAs particularly appealing for individuals seeking stable, predictable income in retirement without exposing themselves to the full risks of the stock market.

At its core, an FIA functions as a contract between you and an insurance company. You make a lump sum payment or a series of payments, and in return, the insurer agrees to provide you with guaranteed benefits. These benefits often include tax-deferred growth, income options, and death benefits for your beneficiaries. Unlike other types of annuities, FIAs allow your account value to grow based on index-linked returns rather than a fixed interest rate or direct stock market investments.

One of the key features of an FIA is its "floor" protection. This means that even if the market index experiences negative returns, your account value will not decrease due to market losses. The trade-off for this protection is that your potential gains are limited by caps, participation rates, or spreads, which we'll discuss in detail shortly.

FIAs are particularly suitable for retirees and pre-retirees who want to:

- Protect their principal from market downturns.
- Participate in some market growth without the risk of direct market investment.
- Create a source of guaranteed income in retirement.
- Plan for legacy or estate purposes by leaving assets to beneficiaries.

While FIAs are not a one-size-fits-all solution, they can play a valuable role in a diversified retirement strategy, particularly when combined with Roth conversions to manage tax liabilities and create tax-efficient income streams.

How Index Crediting Works

The growth of a Fixed Indexed Annuity is tied to the performance of a specific market index, such as the S&P 500, Nasdaq, or Dow Jones Industrial Average. However, it's important to note that you are not directly investing in the index itself. Instead, the insurance company uses the index as a benchmark to determine the amount of interest credited to your account. Let's break down how this works.

Index Crediting Strategies

FIAs offer several index crediting strategies, each with unique features and trade-offs. The most common methods include:

1. **Annual Point-to-Point** This method calculates the change in the index value over a one-year period, comparing the index's starting point to its ending point. The interest credited to your account is based on this change, subject to the terms of the

FIA contract (e.g., caps, participation rates, or spreads).

For example, if the index grows by 8% in a year and your contract has a cap of 6%, you would be credited 6% interest for that year. If the index experiences a loss, no interest is credited, but your account value remains unchanged due to the FIA's floor protection.

2. **Monthly Point-to-Point** In this strategy, the index performance is measured monthly, and the interest credited is based on the sum of the monthly changes over the contract year. Positive months contribute to the total, while negative months may offset gains.

This strategy can provide higher potential returns in a volatile market but may also result in lower returns if negative months are significant.

3. **Monthly Average** The monthly average method calculates the average of the index values over the contract year and compares it to the index's starting value. The interest credited is based on this average change.

This strategy smooths out the impact of market volatility, offering more stable returns over time.

4. **Two-Year or Multi-Year Point-to-Point** Similar to the annual point-to-point method, this strategy measures index performance over a longer period, such as two or more years. While this can result in higher returns during a strong market, it requires a longer commitment and patience to realize potential gains.

Caps, Participation Rates, and Spreads

Basic index crediting in FIAs is subject to certain limitations that balance the insurer's ability to offer downside protection. These limitations include:

1. **Caps** A cap is the maximum interest rate that can be credited to your account during a given period. For example, if your FIA has a cap of 6% and the index grows by 8%, you will only receive 6% interest.

2. **Participation Rates** The participation rate determines the percentage of the index's growth that is credited to your account. For instance, if the participation rate is 80% and the index grows by 10%, your account would be credited with 8% interest (80% of 10%).

3. **Spreads** A spread is a set percentage that is subtracted from the index's growth before calculating the interest credited to your account. For example, if the spread is 2% and the index grows by 10%, you would receive 8% interest (10% - 2%).

These limitations ensure that the insurer can maintain the financial stability needed to honor the guaranteed features of the FIA, such as principal protection and income guarantees.

The Role of the Floor

The floor is a critical feature of FIAs that distinguishes them from direct market investments. If the index experiences a negative return, the floor ensures that no losses are applied to your account value. In other words, your principal is fully protected from market downturns. This guarantees a level of financial security, making FIAs particularly attractive for risk-averse investors.

For example, if the index drops by 15% in a year, your account value remains unchanged. While you won't earn any interest for that year, you also won't lose any of your initial investment or previously credited interest.

Why Understanding Index Crediting Matters

Choosing the right index crediting strategy is essential for optimizing the performance of your FIA. Your decision should align with your financial goals, risk tolerance, and overall retirement strategy. Each individual's circumstances are unique, so it's vital to approach this decision with careful planning and guidance from a knowledgeable financial advisor. They can evaluate the options available and help you select the strategy that best suits your needs and objectives.

Understanding how index crediting works also helps set realistic expectations for growth. While FIAs offer the opportunity to earn interest based on market performance, they are not designed to deliver the same returns as direct stock market investments. Instead, their purpose is to strike a balance between growth potential and the security of principal protection. This makes them an attractive option for retirees and pre-retirees who prioritize stability alongside moderate growth.

One of the key advantages of FIAs is their ability to mitigate the emotional impact of market volatility. Unlike direct investments, which can cause anxiety during market downturns, FIAs provide a safety net with their "floor" feature, ensuring your principal is shielded from losses. This allows you to participate in some market upside without enduring the stress of potential downside risks.

Moreover, selecting the right crediting strategy allows you to tailor the performance of your FIA to match your risk appetite and time horizon. For example, a more conservative investor might favor strategies with a lower cap but higher stability, while someone with a longer time horizon might explore options with higher participation rates for greater growth potential. These customizations make FIAs highly adaptable to varying financial situations.

In summary, understanding index crediting empowers you to make informed decisions and avoid disappointment by setting clear expectations. FIAs are not a "get-rich-quick" solution but rather a measured and secure tool to grow your retirement savings while protecting against market downturns. This balance makes them a valuable component of a well-rounded retirement plan.

In the next section, we'll explore additional features and benefits of FIAs, such as living benefits, death benefits, and how they compare to other types of annuities. By gaining a comprehensive understanding, you can determine if an FIA aligns with your long-term financial goals.

Detailed Understanding: Caps, Participation Rates, and Spreads

When it comes to Fixed Indexed Annuities (FIAs), understanding the mechanics behind caps, participation rates, and spreads is essential for making informed decisions. These features determine how much of the market's growth your annuity will capture. Let's break each of these terms down.

Caps Caps refer to the maximum interest rate your annuity can earn during a given period. For instance, if the cap is set at 5% and the market index grows by 7%, your annuity will only credit 5% for that period. While caps might seem restrictive, they protect you from market downturns. Think of the cap as a trade-off: in exchange for protection against losses, there's a limit to how much you can earn in a booming market.

Uncapped Options Uncapped FIAs, on the other hand, remove these restrictions on earnings and allow you to fully participate in the market's growth potential, minus any applicable spreads or fees. These options are especially appealing for Roth conversions because they maximize the growth of your tax-free funds. By removing the ceiling on returns, uncapped FIAs provide a powerful combination of growth and protection, ensuring your retirement savings are fully optimized.

For example, if an uncapped FIA's index delivers a 12% return in a given year, you would receive the full credit, subject only to the participation rate or spread. This makes uncapped FIAs a preferred choice for retirees looking to offset the tax burden of Roth conversions while building a robust financial legacy.

Participation Rates Participation rates indicate the percentage of the market's growth that your annuity will capture. For example, if the participation rate is 80% and the market index increases by 10%, your annuity will credit 8% (80% of 10%). Some FIAs offer 100% participation, meaning you capture all the growth, subject to the cap or spread. Others might offer higher participation rates but offset them with other limitations.

Consider an example using the BNPIMAD5 index which has an average annual return of 7.28% based on live history. The participation rate in an FIA can vary depending on the term of the annuity contract. For instance, a 7-year term might offer a participation rate of 190%, while a 10-year term could have a participation rate of 145%. This means that with a 7-year term, if the index returns 7.28% in a given year, the realized credited growth would be 13.83% (7.28% × 190%). Similarly, with a 10-year term, the realized credited growth would be 10.55% (7.28% × 145%).

At first glance it would seem that the 7 year annuity is far better than the 10 year just based on this one index return. It's important to evaluate the entire annuity not just one index when making a final judgement. In this case, the 10 year annuity actually provides an 18% premium bonus to help offset the lower indexing rates.

Uncapped participation rates like these are especially beneficial for Roth conversions, as they allow for significant tax-free growth on converted funds. By choosing an FIA with high participation rates, retirees can maximize their growth potential while maintaining protection against market downturns.

Example of Par and Cap Rates:

Fixed Index Account Rates

Some strategies may not be available in all states. Please filter for your state to see approved strategies.	Current Rates 10/25/2024			Guaranteed Minimum Values		
	Fee	Cap	Par	Fee	Cap	Par
1 Year AI Powered Global Opportunities	-		100.00	-	-	10
1 Year AI Powered Global Opportunities with Charge	1.25		140.00	-	-	10
1 Year S&P 500 FC	-		66.00	-	-	10
1 Year S&P 500 FC with Charge	1.25		90.00	-	-	10
1 Year UBS Innovative Balanced	-		100.00	-	-	10
1 Year UBS Innovative Balanced with Charge	1.25		140.00	-	-	10
1-Year AI Powered US Equity Index	-		115.00	-	-	10
1-Year AI Powered US Equity Index With Charge	1.25		140.00	1.25	-	10
1-Year BNP Paribas Multi-Asset No Cap Point-to-Point	-		145.00	-	-	10
1-Year BNP Paribas Multi-Asset No Cap Point-to-Point With Charge	1.25		200.00	1.25	-	10
1-Year Nasdaq FC Index	-		82.00	-	-	10
1-Year Nasdaq FC Index With Charge	1.25		115.00	1.25	-	10
1-Year S&P 500 Point-to-Point Cap Index Strategy With Charge	1.25	8.50		1.25	0.50	-
1-Year S&P 500 Point-to-Point Cap Strategy	-	6.00		-	0.50	-
2 Year AI Powered Global Opportunities	-		135.00	-	-	10
2 Year AI Powered Global Opportunities with Charge	1.25		190.00	-	-	10
2 Year S&P 500 FC	-		90.00	-	-	10
2 Year S&P 500 FC with Charge	1.25		125.00	-	-	10
2 Year UBS Innovative Balanced	-		135.00	-	-	10
2 Year UBS Innovative Balanced with Charge	1.25		190.00	-	-	10
2-Year AI Powered US Equity Index	-		155.00	-	-	10
2-Year AI Powered US Equity Index With Charge	1.25		215.00	1.25	-	10
2-Year BNP Paribas Multi-Asset No Cap Point-to-Point	-		195.00	-	-	10
2-Year BNP Paribas Multi-Asset No Cap Point-to-Point With Charge	1.25		270.00	1.25	-	10
2-Year Nasdaq FC Index	-		130.00	-	-	10
2-Year Nasdaq FC Index With Charge	1.25		175.00	1.25	-	10

Spreads Spreads work differently from caps and participation rates. Instead of setting a maximum or percentage of growth, a spread deducts a fixed percentage from the index's growth. For example, if the spread is 2% and the market grows by 8%, your credited growth will be 6% (8% minus 2%). Spreads are less common than caps or participation rates but are another way insurers manage risk.

Example of Cap and Spreads:

Interest Rate History

		[illegible]	[illegible]	[illegible]	[illegible]	1/10/24	[illegible]	4/9/24	5/8/24	8/14/24	9/13/24	11/11/24	1/6/25
1 Year S&P 500 Annual Point to Point with Cap	Cap	8.50	8.50	8.50	6.50	6.75	6.75	6.75	7.00	6.50	6.50	6.50	6.50
1 Year S&P 500 Annual Point to Point with Participation Rate	Par	47	47	47	47	47	47	47	47	42	42	42	42
1 Year S&P 500 Monthly Cap	Cap	2.75	2.75	2.75	2.75	2.25	2.25	2.25	2.50	2.15	2.15	2.15	2.15
1 Year S&P 500 Monthly Average with Participation Rate	Par	80	80	80	80	80	80	80	80	80	80	80	80
1 Year Barclays Atlas 5 Annual Point to Point Participation Rate	Par	195	195	195	195	162	162	162	165	152	152	152	152
1 Year S&P 500 RavenPack AI w/Participation	Par	210	210	210	210	172	172	172	175	162	162	162	162
1 Year S&P 500 RavenPack AI w/Spread	Spread	-4.25	-4.25	-4.25	-4.25	-3.00	-3.00	-3.00	-3.25	-2.50	-2.50	-2.50	-2.50
1 Year Barclays Atlas 5 Point-to-Point w/Spread	Spread	-4.00	-4.00	-4.00	4.00	2.75	2.75	2.75	2.75	2.25	2.25	2.25	2.25
NASDAQ Generations 5 w/Participation	Par	195	195	195	195	167	167	167	170	157	157	157	157
NASDAQ Generations 5 w/Spread	Spread	-4.00	4.00	-4.00	-4.00	-2.75	2.75	-2.75	-3.00	2.25	2.25	-2.25	2.25
1 Year S&P DynSaff Point-to-Point w/Participation	Par	75	75	75	75	60	60	60	62	57	57	57	57

Balancing the Elements Understanding these mechanisms is crucial because they determine how much your FIA can grow over time. For retirees focused on Roth conversions, this growth directly impacts the tax-free income available later. When comparing different FIAs, pay close attention to how these features align with your retirement goals. A lower cap may be acceptable if you prioritize stability, whereas a higher participation rate might appeal if you're willing to take on a bit more variability for potential growth.

Premium Bonuses

A premium bonus is an incentive offered by some annuities, where the insurance company adds a percentage (e.g., 5% to 20%) to the initial deposit to boost the contract value. This bonus is especially common in Fixed Indexed Annuities (FIAs) and variable annuities and is designed to enhance long-term growth or increase the income base for Guaranteed Lifetime Withdrawal Benefits (GLWB).

However, premium bonuses often come with trade-offs, such as longer surrender periods, higher fees, lower participation rates, or reduced caps on market-linked growth. While they can be beneficial for long-term retirement income, it's essential to evaluate whether the bonus outweighs potential limitations within the annuity contract.

Example Premium Bonus: State regulated bonuses are a way to lock in your return on investment without having to wait to see what the market does.

Premium Bonus

All Other States	
	20.00
CT ID LA MD MN NJ NV OH OK OR PA SC TX UT WA	
	18.00
Indiana	
	20.00
Delaware	
	8.00
Alaska	
	10.00
Florida	
Ages 0-64	20.00
Ages 65-78	18.00

Example 2: Some carriers offer bigger bonuses for larger contract values.

Premium Bonus

$ 20,000+ Band

Year	1	2	3
Rate	10.00	10.00	10.00
With Rider	Add up to 12.0		

$ 75,000+ Band

Year	1	2	3
Rate	14.00	14.00	14.00
With Rider	Add up to 12.0		

Hypothetical Case Study: Janet's Roth Conversion Strategy Using a Fixed Indexed Annuity

Background:
Janet, a 62-year-old retiree, is looking for a tax-efficient way to convert her traditional IRA to a Roth IRA while ensuring steady, tax-free growth and minimizing market risk. After reviewing different options, she decides to use a Fixed Indexed Annuity (FIA) as part of her Roth conversion strategy.

FIA Selection:

- Cap Rate: 5%
- Participation Rate: 80%
- Index Growth Assumption: 6% per year
- Premium Bonus: 16% (applied upfront to the initial investment)
- Conversion Amount: $300,000

- Tax Rate on Conversion: 24%

Step 1: Applying the Premium Bonus
Janet's FIA comes with a 16% premium bonus, meaning that when she deposits her $300,000, she receives an additional $48,000 (16% of $300,000).
Total Starting Annuity Value =

$300,000+$48,000=$348,000

Step 2: Growth Calculations Over 5 Years
Janet's annuity earns interest based on the index performance with an **80% participation rate.**
Annual Growth Calculation:
The assumed index return is **6% annually**. With an 80% participation rate:

6%×0.80=4.8%

Each year, her annuity credits **4.8% growth** (assuming it reaches the cap each year).

Year-by-Year Annuity Growth:

Year	Starting Balance	Growth (%)	Growth ($)	New Balance
1	$348,000	4.8%	$16,704	$364,704
2	$364,704	4.8%	$17,491	$382,195
3	$382,195	4.8%	$18,134	$400,329
4	$400,329	4.8%	$19,215	$419,544
5	$419,544	4.8%	$20,136	$439,680

Total FIA Value After 5 Years: $439,680

Step 3: Covering the Tax Liability Using the FIA Bonus and Growth
Since Janet is converting $300,000 to a Roth IRA, she needs to pay taxes upfront.

- Tax Due: $300,000 × 24% = $72,000
- Bonus Received: $48,000
- Shortfall (Tax Due - Bonus): $72,000 - $48,000 = $24,000

To cover this remaining $24,000 tax liability, Janet can use the interest earned in the first two years from her FIA while keeping her original investment intact.

Step 4: Roth IRA Growth Potential After 5 Years
Since Janet converted $300,000 to a Roth IRA, that money grows tax-free. Assuming the same 6% index return and an 80% participation rate (4.8% growth annually), the Roth IRA grows as follows:

Year	Starting Roth Balance	Growth (%)	Growth ($)	New Roth Balance
1	$300,000	4.8%	$14,400	$314,400
2	$314,400	4.8%	$15,091	$329,491
3	$329,491	4.8%	$15,815	$345,306
4	$345,306	4.8%	$16,575	$361,881
5	$361,881	4.8%	$17,369	$379,250

Total Roth IRA Value After 5 Years: $379,250 (Tax-Free Money!)

Final Outcome for Janet
After five years, Janet achieves:
FIA Account Value: $439,680 (growth + original investment)
Roth IRA Value: $379,250 (grows tax-free)
Taxes Paid Using FIA Bonus & Growth: Covered fully by the bonus and early interest
Key Takeaways:

- Janet offsets $48,000 of her tax bill with the FIA bonus.
- By leveraging FIA growth, she covers the remaining tax liability of $24,000 within two years.
- Her Roth IRA grows tax-free to nearly $380,000 after five years.
- Meanwhile, her FIA grows to over $439,000, ensuring additional financial security.

This strategy protects Janet from market downturns, eliminates RMDs, and ensures a tax-free inheritance for her heirs.

Why This Strategy Works for Roth Conversions:

✓ Mitigates tax liability with FIA premium bonuses.
✓ Provides growth without market risk using the FIA.
✓ Locks in tax-free income for life with the Roth IRA.
✓ Avoids Required Minimum Distributions (RMDs).

Living Benefits and Death Benefits

FIAs are more than just tax-efficient growth vehicles; they also offer living and death benefits that provide added security and flexibility. These features address two critical concerns for retirees: ensuring income for life and leaving a legacy for loved ones.

Living Benefits One of the most attractive features of FIAs is the optional living benefit rider. These riders guarantee a stream of income for life, regardless of how long you live or how the market performs. The most common type is a Guaranteed Lifetime Withdrawal Benefit (GLWB), which ensures you receive a fixed annual income even if your account balance runs out. For retirees concerned about outliving their savings, this can be a game-changer.

Living benefits often include a growth factor for the income base, such as a 5% annual roll-up. This means the income base increases each year you defer withdrawals, up to a certain point. For example, if you invest $200,000 and defer withdrawals for five years, your income base could grow to $255,000. While this growth doesn't directly affect your account value, it determines the amount of guaranteed income you can withdraw.

Death Benefits FIAs also provide death benefits, ensuring your beneficiaries receive the remaining account value if you pass away. Some FIAs offer enhanced death benefit riders, which might include features like:

1. **Guaranteed Payouts:** A guaranteed payout amount, regardless of market performance.

2. **Growth Factors:** Additional growth for the death benefit value, often tied to a fixed rate or index performance.

3. **Flexibility:** Options for lump-sum payouts or annuitized payments over time.

Death benefits are especially valuable in Roth conversion strategies because they transfer tax-free to heirs, maximizing the legacy you leave behind.

Example Death Benefit:

[illegible]

Hypothetical Case Study: Tom and Sarah's Roth Conversion Strategy Using a Fixed Indexed Annuity (FIA)

Background:
Tom and Sarah, both 57, were planning for their retirement and wanted a strategy that would provide **guaranteed lifetime income, tax-free growth, and financial security for their heirs**. They were particularly concerned about future **tax increases, Required Minimum Distributions (RMDs), and ensuring a lasting financial legacy**.

After evaluating their options, they decided to **convert $300,000 from their traditional IRA into a Fixed Indexed Annuity (FIA)** with a **Guaranteed Lifetime Withdrawal Benefit (GLWB) rider** and **an enhanced death benefit**. Their goal was to defer withdrawals until **age 62** to maximize their income potential.

Step 1: Applying the Premium Bonus
Their FIA included a **6% premium bonus**, which immediately increased their **initial deposit of $300,000** by **$18,000**, bringing their starting accumulation value to **$318,000**.

Total Starting Annuity Value:

$300,000+$18,000=$318,000

This bonus helps offset the **Roth conversion tax liability** and provides a larger base for tax-free growth.

Step 2: Growth During the Deferral Period

From **age 57 to 62**, their annuity benefited from index credits and roll-up increases from the GLWB rider. Assuming **a 6% roll-up rate**, their **income base grew to approximately $375,000** by the time they were ready to start withdrawals at age 62.

Projected Income Base Growth (Guaranteed Roll-Up):

$$\$318{,}000 \times (1.06)^5 = \$375{,}000$$

Step 3: Guaranteed Lifetime Income Starts at Age 62

At **age 62**, Tom and Sarah began taking **guaranteed lifetime income withdrawals of $26,384 per year**. These withdrawals were calculated based on the **income base of $375,000** and their annuity's payout factor.

Annual Lifetime Income:

$$\$375{,}000 \times \text{withdrawal factor} = \$26{,}384 \text{ at age 62}$$

This income stream continued **for both of their lifetimes**, ensuring **financial security** regardless of market conditions.

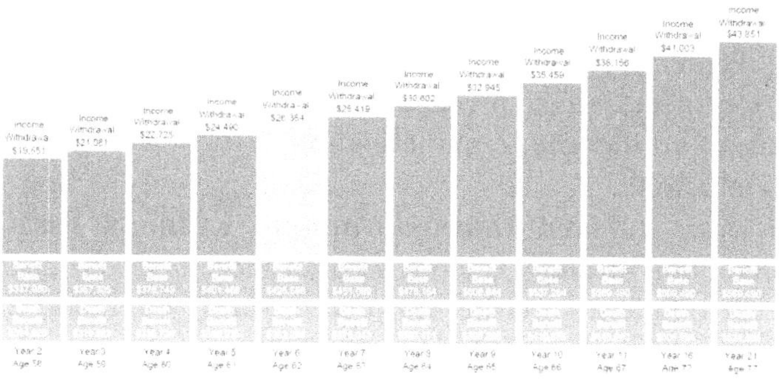

Step 4: Survivor Benefits and Wealth Transfer

When Tom **passed away at age 80**, Sarah **continued receiving the same annual income of $26,384** for the rest of her life. This guaranteed income provided her with financial **peace of mind** and eliminated the risk of outliving her savings.

Upon Sarah's passing, their **children inherited the remaining annuity account value**, which had been growing tax-free. Since the annuity was structured within a **Roth IRA**, their heirs received the funds **completely tax-free**, preserving their family's financial legacy.

Key Benefits of Their Strategy:

✅ **Tax-Free Growth & Income** – Their annuity grew **tax-free** within the Roth IRA, eliminating taxes on future withdrawals.

✅ **Avoided RMDs** – Unlike a traditional IRA, their Roth conversion strategy meant **no forced withdrawals at age 75**.

✅ **Guaranteed Income for Life** – Their **$26,384 annual withdrawal** was **guaranteed for both spouses**, regardless of market fluctuations.

✅ **Enhanced Death Benefit** – Their children **inherited the remaining account value tax-free**, ensuring a **lasting financial legacy**.

✅ **Protection Against Market Downturns** – Since the FIA protected their principal from market losses, their **retirement income remained stable**.

Conclusion:

By using a **Fixed Indexed Annuity within a Roth conversion strategy**, Tom and Sarah successfully created a **tax-efficient, market-protected, and guaranteed income plan** that ensured financial **security for their lifetime and a tax-free inheritance for their heirs**.

Fees and Surrender Charges

While FIAs offer many benefits, it's essential to understand the associated fees and surrender charges. These costs can impact your overall returns and liquidity.

Understanding Fees Most FIAs have no direct fees for the base product, but optional riders, such as living or death benefit riders, often come with additional costs. These fees are typically deducted annually from the account value and can range from 0.5% to 1.5%. For example, if your account value is $200,000 and the rider fee is 1%, you'll pay $2,000 annually.

While fees might seem like a drawback, they often provide valuable guarantees, such as lifetime income, an upfront bonus or enhanced death benefits. It's crucial to weigh the cost against the benefits when selecting riders.

Surrender Charges Surrender charges apply if you withdraw more than the penalty-free amount or cancel the annuity during the surrender period. These charges typically start high, around 7-10%, and decrease over time, usually over 5-10 years. For example, if you withdraw $50,000 in the first year and the surrender charge is 8%, you'll lose $4,000 to penalties.

Many FIAs allow penalty-free withdrawals of up to 10% of the account value each year, providing some liquidity without triggering surrender charges. However, exceeding this limit or withdrawing during the early years can be costly.

How to Manage Costs To minimize fees and surrender charges, consider the following:

1. Choose riders carefully, ensuring they align with your retirement goals.

2. Understand the surrender period and avoid large withdrawals during this time.

3. Opt for FIAs with shorter surrender periods if liquidity is a priority.

Examples of Surrender Charges from different carriers

This example shows a 10-year annuity with a 9 year surrender charge.

[illegible]	[illegible]	[illegible]	[illegible]	[illegible]	[illegible]	[illegible]	[illegible]	[illegible]	[illegible]
[illegible]	[illegible]	[illegible]	[illegible]	[illegible]	[illegible]	[illegible]	[illegible]	[illegible]	[illegible]

Surrender Charges

Some states cap surrender charges for annuity contracts.

[illegible]	[illegible]	[illegible]	[illegible]	[illegible]	[illegible]	[illegible]	[illegible]	[illegible]	[illegible]	[illegible]
[illegible]	[illegible]	[illegible]	[illegible]	[illegible]	[illegible]	[illegible]	[illegible]	[illegible]	[illegible]	[illegible]
[illegible]	[illegible]	[illegible]	[illegible]	[illegible]	[illegible]	[illegible]	[illegible]	[illegible]	[illegible]	[illegible]

Surrender Charges

Surrender charges are monitored and regulated by individual states and may vary from state to state and by age of the owner of the annuity at the start of the contract.

Surrender Charges

Year	1	2	3	4	5	6	7	8	9	10
AK CT DE ID LA MN NJ NV OH OK OR PA SC TX UT WA	8.30	8.00	7.10	6.20	5.30	4.40	3.50	2.60	1.60	0.90
Maryland	10.00	10.00	10.00	10.00	9.00	8.00	7.00	6.00	4.00	-
Florida	-	-	-	-	-	-	-	-	-	-
Ages 0-64	12.00	12.00	12.00	11.00	10.00	9.00	8.00	7.00	6.00	4.00
Ages 65-78	10.00	10.00	10.00	10.00	9.00	8.00	7.00	6.00	5.00	4.00
All Other States	12.00	12.00	12.00	11.00	10.00	9.00	8.00	7.00	6.00	4.00

Linda's Experience with a Fixed Indexed Annuity

Background:

At **age 63**, Linda invested **$250,000** into a **Fixed Indexed Annuity (FIA)** with a **10-year surrender period**. To secure guaranteed lifetime income, she added a **Guaranteed Lifetime Withdrawal Benefit (GLWB) rider**, which came with an **annual fee of 0.95%**. Linda's strategy was to **withdraw 10% of her account value annually**, ensuring she stayed within the **penalty-free withdrawal limit** while allowing her remaining balance to grow. This gave her a lot more income than the projected 4% withdrawal which is typical of a stock or bond portfolio.

Growth, Fees, and Withdrawals Over Time:

- **Growth Assumption:** Linda's annuity was projected to grow at **5% annually**.

- **Annual Fee:** Each year, **0.95%** was deducted from the total account value to cover the rider.

- **Withdrawals:** She withdrew **10% annually**, ensuring she avoided **surrender charges** while benefiting from guaranteed income.

Over **15 years**, Linda withdrew a **significant portion of her annuity** while maintaining a balance that continued to grow due to compounding interest. However, as the account balance declined due to withdrawals and fees, her **growth eventually slowed**, and the fees began to take a larger percentage of her remaining funds.

Break-Even Point on the Annual Fee:

- In the **early years**, her **5% growth outpaced** the **0.95% fee**, allowing her balance to remain strong.

- By **year 10**, the combination of **withdrawals and fees** started to outweigh the growth.

- By **year 15**, her remaining balance had **declined significantly** due to continuous withdrawals and fees.

Final Outcome:

Linda successfully executed her strategy by **maximizing penalty-free withdrawals** while still growing her account in the early years. Linda's **FIA strategy** (with a **10% withdrawal rate**) allowed her to withdraw a **total of $255,655** over 15 years.

If she had used a **traditional 4% withdrawal strategy**, she would have been able to withdraw only **$154,294** over the same period.

This means the **FIA strategy provided an additional $101,360 in withdrawals** over 15 years compared to the traditional 4% withdrawal approach.

However, the trade-off is that the FIA account value declined faster due to the **higher withdrawal rate** and **annual rider fees**. In contrast, the **traditional 4% withdrawal approach preserved more of the account balance** over time. Linda understood that while her retirement income was able to remain stable throughout her lifetime the amount she was leaving behind to her beneficiaries was declining.

Key Takeaways:

✅ **10% withdrawals allowed penalty-free access to funds**

✅ **The 0.95% fee was manageable in the early years but became more impactful over time**

✅ **Growth initially outpaced the fee but eventually slowed as withdrawals reduced the account balance**

✅ **Linda enjoyed financial security in retirement with guaranteed income for life.**

Comparing FIAs to Other Annuity Types

FIAs are just one of many annuity types available, each with its unique features and benefits. To understand why FIAs are often a popular choice for Roth conversions, let's compare them to other annuities.

Variable Annuities (VAs) Variable annuities invest your premiums in market-based portfolios, offering potentially higher growth but exposing you to market risk and annual fees that are typically in the 3% to 5% range. Unlike FIAs, VAs don't guarantee protection against losses. While they may appeal to more aggressive investors, VAs lack the stability that many retirees prefer.

Immediate Annuities Immediate annuities provide guaranteed income starting right away. While they're great for securing immediate cash flow, they don't offer growth potential or flexibility. FIAs, on the other hand, allow you to grow your funds while deferring income, making them better suited for long-term planning.

Traditional Fixed Annuities Traditional fixed annuities guarantee a fixed interest rate for a set period. These are used an alternative for Certificates of Deposit (CD's) in a portfolio. While they offer stability, they lack the growth potential of FIAs. For retirees seeking a balance between safety and growth, FIAs are often the better choice.

Why FIAs Stand Out FIAs combine the best of both worlds: protection against market losses and the potential for growth. They offer:

1. **Index-Linked Growth:** Unlike fixed annuities, FIAs grow based on index performance, providing higher earning potential.

2. **Downside Protection:** Unlike VAs, FIAs protect your principal from market downturns.

3. **Flexibility:** FIAs allow you to defer income and customize features with optional riders.

Case Study: Bill's Choice Bill, a 70-year-old retiree, compared a Variable Annuity (VA), a Fixed Annuity, and a Fixed Indexed Annuity (FIA) to determine which was best suited for his Roth Conversion. His primary concern was protecting his savings from market volatility, which led him to rule out the VA despite its potential for higher growth. Immediate annuities, while offering immediate payouts, didn't align with his desire to let his funds grow for a few more years.

After thorough research, Bill opted for an FIA designed for growth, featuring historical indexing returns in the 5% to 12% range. This FIA also included an upfront premium bonus of 10%, which Bill used to offset the taxes from his Roth conversion. By leveraging the premium bonus, Bill was able to reduce the immediate tax burden while positioning his funds for significant growth over the long term. Over the next 10 years, the annuity's indexed growth consistently delivered returns within the historical range, allowing Bill's Roth-converted funds to grow tax-free. The combination of strong growth potential and the upfront bonus ensured Bill could maximize his retirement savings and achieve his long-term financial goals.

Bill's strategy also accounted for his long-term needs. By selecting a growth-oriented FIA, Bill ensured that his retirement nest egg was protected during periods when the market did not perform well, while still allowing him to participate in market growth with unlimited upside potential. This FIA provided historical indexing returns ranging from 5% to 12%, enabling Bill's funds to grow tax-free over time. The added protection from market losses gave Bill peace of mind, while the unlimited upside potential ensured that he could take advantage of market gains without worrying about caps. Additionally, the FIA included a death benefit, allowing his heirs to inherit the remaining value tax-free, aligning perfectly with his goal of leaving a legacy.

By understanding the nuances of caps, participation rates, and spreads, the benefits of living and death benefits, the impact of fees and surrender charges, and how FIAs compare to other annuity types, retirees can make informed decisions. FIAs are powerful tools for Roth conversions, providing growth, stability, and peace of mind.

PART II: THE STRATEGY

Chapter 3: The FIA-Roth Conversion Strategy

Overview of the Combined Strategy

The FIA-Roth Conversion Strategy combines two powerful financial tools—Fixed Indexed Annuities (FIAs) and Roth conversions—to help retirees optimize their retirement savings while minimizing tax liabilities. This strategy is particularly beneficial for those nearing or in retirement who are concerned about rising taxes, market volatility, and the risk of outliving their savings. By leveraging the unique features of FIAs, such as tax-deferred growth, market-linked returns, premium, roll up or beneficiary bonuses, and guaranteed income options, retirees can confidently navigate the complexities of converting their traditional retirement accounts to Roth IRAs. There are multiple ways to design the Roth Conversion using a Fixed Indexed Annuity, and this book will focus on only three options:

- **Option 1**: Paying the taxes using "external" monies from a non-qualified checking or savings account. This strategy is used to have the highest balance in the Roth after the conversion as you are preserving the principal in the FIA by not using the principal, bonus or indexing to pay the taxes. You are paying the taxes from a stock account, checking or savings account.

- **Option 2**: Using "internal" funds from the indexing, premium, roll up, or other one-time bonuses to pay the taxes while not depleting the original principal balance. With this option no money needs to be used from an outside stock, checking or savings account so long as the bonus(es) and/or interest are enough to cover the tax liability on the funds being converted.

- **Option 3**: Setting up a Roth conversion for transferring wealth tax-free to kids, grandkids, or other beneficiaries by using a Beneficiary Bonus option. A lucky few have more retirement assets that far exceed their estimated retirement expenses. This results in the principal balance being converted but the bonuses, which can be upwards of 40% of the original premium, are not converted.

The cornerstone of this strategy is its ability to provide a tax-efficient pathway to Roth conversions based on your specific goals of either.

a) converting as much money as possible into the Roth
b) converting the IRA but preserving available cash reserves or
c) converting some money but maximizing the amount of money to be left as an inheritance to your heirs.

While there are many other ways to perform Roth conversion both with and without Fixed Indexed Annuities these are the 3 most popular strategies that are being used today.

Roll Up Bonuses

A roll-up bonus in an annuity is a guaranteed percentage increase applied to the income base, which is used to calculate future withdrawals under a Guaranteed Lifetime Withdrawal Benefit (GLWB) rider. This roll-up typically accrues annually at a fixed rate (e.g., 6% or 8%), compounding over a set period, such as 10 years or until withdrawals begin. Importantly, the roll-up applies only to the income base, not the cash value, meaning it enhances future guaranteed income but does not increase the annuity's lump-sum withdrawal value. This feature is valuable for retirees seeking predictable, lifelong income, as it ensures a growing income stream even if market returns are low.

Example Roll Up Bonuses

Example 1 This carrier offers a 6% bonus every year withdrawals are deferred up to 10 years.

Example 2

Example 3 Roll Up Bonuses can also be regulated by the owner's age.

Issue Age	Bonus	Rollup Rate	Rollup Period	Withdrawal Age	Waiting Period	Fee	Status
[illegible] Max		10% in years 1-10 3% in years 11-20	For 10 years or age 85	[illegible] Min	One year	[illegible]	Required
[illegible] Max		10% in years 1-10 3% in years 11-20	For 10 years or age 85	50 Min	One year	0.35%	Required

Why use a Fixed Indexed Annuity?

Traditional IRAs and 401(k)s are tax-deferred, meaning withdrawals in retirement are taxed as ordinary income. With Roth conversions, retirees pay taxes upfront to enjoy tax-free withdrawals later. However, these taxes can be substantial, especially if conversions are done in a lump sum. This is where FIAs come into play. By offering bonuses, tax-deferred growth, and guaranteed income, FIAs can effectively offset or manage the tax burden associated with Roth conversions.

The FIA-Roth Conversion Strategy also aligns with a broader retirement planning goal: creating a more predictable and secure financial future. Through careful planning and timing, retirees can:

- Lock in lower tax rates today.
- Eliminate Required Minimum Distributions (RMDs) on converted amounts.
- Provide a tax-free inheritance for their heirs.

This chapter will delve into how FIAs complement Roth conversions, offering practical tips, tax-saving strategies, and a detailed case study to illustrate the benefits.

How FIAs Can Help Manage Conversion Taxes

One of the biggest hurdles in Roth conversions is the immediate tax liability. When you convert funds from a traditional IRA or 401(k) to a Roth IRA, the amount converted is treated as taxable income. For many retirees, this sudden increase in taxable income can push them into a higher tax bracket, increase Medicare premiums, and even lead to taxes on Social Security benefits.

FIAs provide a solution to this challenge. Here's how:

1. **Tax-Deferred Growth**: FIAs allow your investments to grow without incurring annual taxes on gains. This tax deferral provides a strategic advantage, enabling retirees to preserve more of their wealth and allocate funds toward conversion taxes.

2. **Premium Bonuses**: Many FIAs offer upfront premium bonuses, which can be as high as 5 to 20% or more. For example, if you invest $500,000 in an FIA with a 10% bonus, you instantly receive an additional $50,000. This bonus can be used strategically to pay for the taxes incurred during a Roth conversion.

3. **Guaranteed Income**: FIAs provide guaranteed lifetime income, ensuring retirees have a steady cash flow to cover living expenses. This frees up other assets that can be allocated toward conversion taxes.

4. **Protection from Market Volatility**: Unlike stocks or mutual funds, FIAs protect your principal from market downturns. This stability ensures that your funds remain intact, giving you more confidence to proceed with Roth conversions.

5. **Income Rider - The Power of Waiting to Start Income**: The Benefit Base is used to determine your Income Withdrawal amount. It is determined by the premiums placed in your annuity compounded annually at 6.00% for up to 10 years.

Delaying the start of Income Withdrawals generally results in a higher Income Withdrawal amount.

By integrating an FIA into your Roth conversion plan, you can minimize the financial strain of paying taxes upfront, ensuring that the long-term benefits of tax-free withdrawals outweigh the initial cost. An experienced retirement specialist should help you in determining the best way to design the plan and what carriers and products to choose.

Using FIA Bonuses and Income to Pay Conversion Taxes

The unique features of FIAs, particularly premium bonuses and guaranteed income streams, make them an ideal tool for funding Roth conversion taxes. Let's explore how these elements work:

1. **Premium Bonuses**: FIA bonuses can significantly reduce the financial burden of Roth conversion taxes. For instance, consider a retiree with $600,000 in a traditional IRA. If they convert $300,000 to a Roth IRA, they may face a tax bill of approximately $75,000 (assuming a 25% tax rate). By investing in an FIA with a 10% bonus, they can generate $60,000 in bonus funds, which can be allocated toward the tax liability. This reduces the out-of-pocket cost, making the conversion more affordable.

2. **Income Riders**: Many FIAs offer optional income riders that provide guaranteed annual payments. These payments can be used to cover taxes incrementally over several years, aligning with a phased Roth conversion strategy. For example, if a retiree receives $30,000 annually from an FIA

income rider, they can use this amount to offset the tax cost of converting $120,000 per year (at a 25% tax rate) over four years.

3. **Strategic Withdrawals**: Some FIAs allow penalty-free withdrawals under specific conditions, such as reaching a certain age. These withdrawals can provide additional liquidity to pay taxes without disrupting the overall retirement plan.

Using FIA bonuses and income to pay conversion taxes not only reduces financial stress but also ensures that retirees maintain their standard of living throughout the process. This strategic use of FIA features allows for a seamless transition to a tax-free retirement.

Timing Your Conversion with FIA Features

Timing is critical when implementing the FIA-Roth Conversion Strategy. Proper timing ensures that retirees can maximize tax savings while minimizing potential pitfalls. Here are key considerations:

1. **Locking in Lower Tax Rates**: With current tax rates set to expire in 2025 under the Tax Cuts and Jobs Act, retirees have a limited window to take advantage of historically low rates. FIAs can provide the necessary financial support to accelerate conversions during this period.

2. **Phased Conversions**: Instead of converting all funds at once, retirees can spread the process over several years, called a partial Roth conversion, to avoid jumping into higher tax brackets. FIAs' income streams can be aligned with this phased approach, providing consistent funding for taxes each year.

3. **Market Volatility**: Converting funds during a market downturn can be advantageous, as lower account values result in smaller taxable amounts. FIAs protect your principal from market losses, ensuring that your retirement funds remain intact and ready for conversion when market conditions stabilize.

4. **Age Considerations**: Timing conversions before age 73 (when RMDs begin) allows retirees to eliminate future RMDs on converted amounts. FIAs' penalty-free withdrawal options and income riders can support this goal.

By aligning Roth conversions with FIA features, retirees can optimize the timing of their strategy, ensuring maximum tax efficiency and financial security.

Case Study: The Smith Family Conversion

To illustrate the benefits of the FIA-Roth Conversion Strategy, let's examine the case of the Smith family:

Background:

- John and Mary Smith, both 62 years old, have $800,000 in a traditional IRA and $300,000 in savings. They are concerned about rising taxes and the potential impact of RMDs on their retirement income. They want to convert $400,000 of their IRA to a Roth IRA over the next four years.

The Strategy:

1. The Smiths invest $500,000 in an FIA with a 10% premium bonus, instantly adding $50,000 to their retirement savings.

2. They use the bonus to cover the first year's Roth conversion tax liability of $25,000, converting $100,000 to a Roth IRA.

3. Over the next three years, they use the FIA's guaranteed income stream of $30,000 annually to fund subsequent tax payments. This allows them to convert an additional $300,000 without dipping into their savings.

The Results:

- The Smiths successfully convert $400,000 to a Roth IRA, locking in today's lower tax rates.

- They eliminate future RMDs on the converted amount, reducing their taxable income in retirement.

- The Roth account grows tax-free, providing a legacy for their children.

- Their remaining IRA funds benefit from the FIA's protection against market volatility and guaranteed income options.

This case study highlights how the FIA-Roth Conversion Strategy can help retirees achieve their financial goals while minimizing tax burdens and preserving their quality of life.

By understanding the synergy between FIAs and Roth conversions, retirees can take actionable steps to secure a tax-free and financially stable retirement. This strategy not only addresses immediate concerns about conversion taxes but also provides long-term benefits, ensuring peace of mind and financial freedom.

PART II: THE STRATEGY

Chapter 4: Tax Considerations

Tax Brackets and Timing

One of the most critical aspects of a successful Roth conversion strategy is understanding tax brackets and timing. Roth conversions involve transferring pre-tax retirement funds, such as those in a traditional IRA or 401(k), into a Roth IRA. During this process, the amount converted is treated as taxable income, which can significantly impact your tax bracket if not planned carefully.

Why Tax Brackets Matter

Tax brackets in the United States are progressive, meaning the more income you earn, the higher the percentage of tax you pay on each additional dollar. For example, if your current taxable income places you in the 22% tax bracket, a Roth conversion could push you into the 24% or even the 32% bracket. This increase in taxable income not only raises your tax liability for the year but can also trigger additional costs, such as higher Medicare premiums and taxation of Social Security benefits.

Timing is Everything

The timing of a Roth conversion is just as important as the amount converted. Ideally, conversions should be executed in years when your taxable income is lower, such as after retirement but before you begin taking Required Minimum Distributions (RMDs) or claim Social Security benefits. These low-income years are often referred to as the "tax sweet spot." Planning your conversions during this period allows you to maximize the amount converted while minimizing the tax impact. Additionally, you may want to consider converting to the top of the tax bracket you are comfortable with each year. Since tax brackets can change annually, reevaluating your strategy every year ensures you stay within your desired limits.

For example, in 2025, the tax brackets are as follows:

2025 Tax Brackets adjusted for inflation in Oct 2024 Verified

Tax rate	Single filers	Married couples filing jointly	Head of household
10%	$0 to $11,925	$0 to $23,850	$16,550 or less
12%	$11,925 to $48,475	$23,850 to $96,950	$16,551 to $63,100
22%	$48,475 to $103,350	$96,950 to $206,700	$63,101 to $100,500
24%	$103,350 to $197,300	$206,700 to $394,600	$100,501 to $191,150
32%	$197,300 to $250,525	$394,600 to $501,050	$191,151 to $243,700
35%	$250,525 to $626,350	$501,050 to $751,600	$243,701 to $609,350
37.0%	$626,350 or more	$751,600 or more	$609,351 or more

The estimated and projected tax brackets for 2026 are as follows:

2026 Tax Brackets These are estimated and will most likely change Not Verified

Tax rate	Single filers	Married couples filing jointly	Head of household
10%	$0 - $9,325	$0 - $18,650	$0 - $13,350
15%	$9,326 - $37,950	$18,651- $75,900	$13,351 - $50,800
25%	$37,951 - $91,900	**$75,901- $153,101**	$50,801- $131,200
28%	$91,901- $191,650	**$153,101- $233,350**	$131,201 - $212,500
33%	$191,651- $416,700	$233,351- $416,700	$212,501- $416,700
35%	$416,701- $418,400	$416,701- $470,700	$416,701- $444,550
39.6%	$418,400 plus	$470,700 plus	$444,550 plus

These brackets are not verified by the IRS. This is assuming the Tax Cut and Jobs Act (TCJA) will not be extended by congress or by executive action before it expires in Dec 2025.

Case Study: Strategic Conversion to Stay Within the 24% Bracket

Imagine Joan, a 62-year-old retiree with $800,000 in a traditional IRA. Her taxable income for the year is $50,000, which places her in the 22% tax bracket. Joan's financial advisor recommends converting $60,000 annually for the next several years to utilize the 24% tax bracket without creeping into the 32% tax bracket. Accounting for growth from interest and any potential bonuses on her investments, it is estimated that it will take Joan approximately 12 to 15 years to fully convert her $800,000 IRA into a Roth IRA.

Alternatively, Joan could use a Fixed Indexed Annuity (FIA) to pay for the taxes on her Roth conversions. By leveraging the bonuses and interest from the FIA, she could convert her entire IRA within 4 to 5 years, staying within the top of the 24% tax bracket. This approach not only accelerates the process but also preserves Joan's cash on hand, as the taxes are effectively covered by the FIA's earnings. This ensures her IRA is fully converted much sooner, giving her more time to enjoy tax-free growth and withdrawals while maintaining her liquid savings for other needs or unexpected expenses. By sticking to either strategy, Joan can achieve her goal of minimizing taxes while maximizing her retirement savings.

IRMAA (Medicare Premium) Implications

What is IRMAA?

The Income-Related Monthly Adjustment Amount (IRMAA) is an additional charge added to Medicare Part B and Part D premiums for higher-income retirees. IRMAA thresholds are determined by your modified adjusted gross income (MAGI) from two years prior. For example, your 2025 IRMAA is based on your 2023 MAGI. While IRMAA can increase Medicare premiums slightly, it's important to consider this as a minor tradeoff compared to the significant tax savings and additional growth potential on Roth-converted funds. The long-term benefits of tax-free growth and withdrawals often outweigh the short-term impact of a slightly higher IRMAA adjustment.

How Roth Conversions Impact IRMAA

A Roth conversion increases your taxable income for the year, which could push you above the IRMAA thresholds. Even a small increase in income could result in significantly higher Medicare premiums. For instance, in 2025, retirees with a MAGI exceeding $97,000 (single filers) or $194,000 (married filing jointly) would face additional Part B and Part D costs.

Mitigating IRMAA Risks

To avoid IRMAA surcharges, consider:

- **Partial Conversions:** Break your Roth conversions into smaller, annual conversions that keep your MAGI below the IRMAA threshold.

- **Income Management:** Time other taxable events, such as capital gains realizations, to avoid compounding your taxable income in a single year.

Case Study: Avoiding the IRMAA Surcharge

Tom and Susan, a married couple, plan to convert $100,000 from their traditional IRA into a Roth IRA in 2025. Their 2023 MAGI was $180,000, just below the IRMAA threshold for joint filers. Their advisor recommends splitting the conversion over two years, converting $50,000 annually to stay within the limits and avoid surcharges.

The 2025 Income-Related Monthly Adjusted Amount IRMAA brackets for Medicare Part B

Full Part B Coverage

Beneficiaries who file individual tax returns with modified adjusted gross income:	Beneficiaries who file joint tax returns with modified adjusted gross income:	Income-Related Monthly Adjustment Amount	Total Monthly Premium Amount
Less than or equal to $106,000	Less than or equal to $212,000	$0.00	$185.00
Greater than $106,000 and less than or equal to $133,000	Greater than $212,000 and less than or equal to $266,000	74.00	259.00
Greater than $133,000 and less than or equal to $167,000	Greater than $266,000 and less than or equal to $334,000	185.00	370.00
Greater than $167,000 and less than or equal to $200,000	Greater than $334,000 and less than or equal to $400,000	295.90	480.90
Greater than $200,000 and less than $500,000	Greater than $400,000 and less than $750,000	406.90	591.90
Greater than or equal to $500,000	Greater than or equal to $750,000	443.90	628.90

Courtesy: CMS.gov
https://www.cms.gov/newsroom/fact-sheets/2025-medicare-parts-b-premiums-and-deductibles

---

State Tax Considerations

State Tax Implications of Roth Conversions

While federal taxes are the primary focus for most retirees, state taxes can also play a significant role in Roth conversion planning. Some states fully tax Roth conversions as income, while others offer partial exemptions or no tax at all.

Tax-Friendly States

If you live in a state with no income tax, such as Florida, Texas, or Nevada, you won't pay state taxes on your Roth conversion. However, if you reside in a high-tax state like California or New York, the additional income could significantly increase your overall tax burden.

Strategies for Minimizing State Taxes

1. **Relocating:** Consider moving to a tax-friendly state before initiating large conversions.

2. **Timing:** Spread conversions over multiple years to avoid substantial one-year tax hits.

3. **Deductions and Credits:** Leverage any state-specific deductions or credits to offset the tax impact.

Case Study: Relocation for Tax Savings
Barbara, a 67-year-old retiree, has $1 million in her IRA and plans to convert $500,000 to a Roth IRA. Living in California, she would face a 13.3% state tax on the conversion. By relocating to Nevada before the conversion, which she had planned to do anyway, Barbara saves $66,500 in state taxes.

Required Minimum Distributions (RMDs)
As of 2025, the **Required Minimum Distribution (RMD)** rules have undergone significant changes due to recent legislation, notably the **SECURE Act of 2019** and the **SECURE 2.0 Act of 2022**. Here's an overview of the current RMD regulations:

1. Starting Age for RMDs

- **Born in 1951 or Later**: Individuals who turn **73** in 2024 are required to take their first RMD by **April 1, 2025**.

- **Born in 1960 or Later**: The RMD starting age increases to **75**, effective January 1, 2033.

2. Inherited IRAs and the 10-Year Rule

For non-spouse beneficiaries inheriting IRAs from individuals who had already begun taking RMDs:

- **Annual Withdrawals**: Beneficiaries must take annual distributions starting by **2025** and fully deplete the account within **10 years** of the original owner's death.

- **Exceptions**: Certain beneficiaries, such as surviving spouses, minor children, and disabled individuals, may have different requirements.

3. Penalties for Missed RMDs

- **Penalty Rate**: Failing to withdraw the full RMD amount by the deadline results in a **25% excise tax** on the undistributed portion.

- **Reduced Penalty**: If corrected within two years, the penalty decreases to **10%**.

4. Qualified Charitable Distributions (QCDs)

- **Age Requirement**: Individuals aged **70½** or older can make QCDs.

- **Limit**: Up to **$100,000** per year can be transferred directly from an IRA to a qualified charity, satisfying part or all of the RMD requirement.

5. Roth IRAs

- **Original Owners**: Roth IRAs do not require RMDs during the owner's lifetime.

- **Beneficiaries**: Inherited Roth IRAs are subject to RMD rules, requiring the account to be emptied within **10 years** of the original owner's death.

It's essential to stay updated on these regulations, as the IRS has indicated that final RMD rules will apply starting in **2026**, potentially introducing further changes.

How Roth Conversions Solve the RMD Problem

Roth IRAs are not subject to RMDs during your lifetime, allowing your investments to grow tax-free indefinitely. By converting funds to a Roth IRA before RMDs begin, you can reduce or eliminate the impact of RMDs on your taxable income. This benefit is outlined under IRS Code Section 408A, which specifies the rules governing Roth IRAs and their exemption from RMD requirements during the account owner's lifetime.

Case Study: Eliminating RMDs with a Roth Conversion

John, a 70-year-old retiree, has $900,000 in his traditional IRA. His RMDs will start at age 73 and are projected to be $40,000 annually. By converting $300,000 to a Roth IRA over three years, John reduces his future RMDs to $25,000 annually, lowering his taxable income and preserving his assets for future growth.

Social Security Tax Impact

How Social Security Benefits are Taxed

Social Security benefits become taxable when your combined income exceeds certain thresholds. Combined income includes your adjusted gross income (AGI), non-taxable interest, and half of your Social Security benefits. Roth conversions increase your AGI, which could make your benefits taxable.

Strategies to Minimize Social Security Taxation

1. **Pre-Claim Conversions:** Complete Roth conversions before claiming Social Security benefits to avoid higher combined income.

2. **Incremental Conversions:** Spread conversions over several years to minimize the impact on your AGI.

Case Study: Managing Social Security Taxation

Emma, a 65-year-old retiree, plans to claim Social Security at age 67. Her advisor recommends converting $40,000 annually for two years before she starts receiving benefits. While it's generally best to start Roth conversions early, ideally before age 65, doing them later is still better than not doing them at all. This strategy minimizes her AGI and keeps her benefits tax-free, demonstrating the value of Roth conversions even at a later stage in retirement planning.

Multi-Year Conversion Strategies

Why a Multi-Year Approach Works

A multi-year conversion strategy allows you to spread the tax liability over several years, avoiding large one-time tax hits and reducing the risk of triggering higher brackets, IRMAA surcharges, or Social Security taxation.

Planning Your Conversions

1. **Calculate Your Sweet Spot:** Work with a financial advisor to determine the optimal conversion amount based on your income, expenses, and tax bracket. Additionally, consider the Rule of 72, a quick and useful formula to estimate the number of years required to double your invested money at a given annual rate of

return. For example, if your portfolio grows at an annual rate of 6%, it will double in approximately 12 years (72 divided by 6). Retirees should keep this in mind because a $1 million portfolio could grow into a $3 or $4 million RMD or tax headache in their 70s or 80s. Balancing conversions to the top of a comfortable tax bracket while considering potential growth is key to managing future tax burdens effectively.

2. **Monitor Legislative Changes:** Stay informed about tax law changes that could impact conversion strategies, such as adjustments to tax brackets or RMD rules. For example, the Tax Cuts and Jobs Act (TCJA) of 2017, signed by President Trump, reduced tax rates and expanded tax brackets. However, these provisions are set to expire at the end of 2025 unless action is taken to extend them. This pending change makes it even more crucial to plan conversions strategically while current tax rates remain in effect.

Case Study: A Five-Year Conversion Plan

Mark, a 60-year-old retiree, has $750,000 in a traditional IRA. His advisor recommends converting $50,000 annually for five years, staying within the 22% tax bracket. This approach allows Mark to convert $250,000 to a Roth IRA while keeping his tax liability manageable. However, it's important to note that you don't need to convert every last penny of your retirement savings. Typical guidance suggests converting to the top of the tax bracket you're comfortable with, converting as much as you can while keeping as much as you can in the Roth, and balancing that with maintaining sufficient cash on hand for immediate needs.

Tools for Success

Use tax projection software or consult a tax professional to simulate various conversion scenarios and choose the most effective strategy for your situation.

By understanding and addressing these tax considerations, you can maximize the benefits of a Roth conversion while minimizing potential pitfalls. With careful planning and expert guidance, a Roth conversion can be a powerful tool for securing a tax-free retirement.

PART III: IMPLEMENTATION

Chapter 5: Step-by-Step Implementation Guide

Evaluating Your Current Situation

Before embarking on a Roth conversion, the first and most important step is evaluating your current financial situation. This means taking a detailed inventory of your retirement accounts, income sources, tax liabilities, and financial goals. Think of this as creating a financial snapshot that will guide your decisions.

Start by asking yourself the following:

- What is the total value of my IRA or 401(k)?
- How much income do I expect in retirement, including Social Security, pensions, and other sources?
- What is my current tax bracket, and how might it change in the coming years?
- Are there other tax considerations, such as deductions, credits, or Medicare premiums, that could impact my strategy?

Begin by gathering all your account statements. Review balances, contribution limits, and any existing Roth accounts. If you have multiple IRAs or 401(k)s, consolidate this information into a single spreadsheet or document. This will make it easier to analyze your overall situation and identify opportunities for tax-efficient conversions.

It's also critical to consider your time horizon. If you're closer to retirement, the window to execute a Roth conversion may be narrower. On the other hand, if you're still several years away, you may have the flexibility to spread out conversions and minimize your annual tax burden.

Finally, assess any potential risks. For example, if market volatility has impacted your retirement accounts, it might be advantageous to convert during a downturn when your account values are lower, thus reducing the taxable amount of your conversion.

Choosing the Right FIA

Fixed Indexed Annuities (FIAs) are a powerful tool for retirees seeking stability and growth potential while implementing a Roth conversion. However, not all FIAs are created equal. Choosing the right FIA is critical to ensuring your strategy works effectively.

Start by understanding the basic features of an FIA:

- **Principal Protection:** Your investment is protected from market losses.

- **Index-Linked Growth:** FIAs offer the potential for growth by tracking a market index, such as the S&P 500, without directly investing in the market.

- **Guaranteed Lifetime Income:** Many FIAs include riders that provide guaranteed income for life, which can alleviate concerns about outliving your savings.

When selecting an FIA, pay attention to the following factors:

1. **Caps and Participation Rates:** These dictate how much of the index's growth you can capture. Higher caps and participation rates typically translate to greater growth potential.

2. **Fees:** While FIAs often have lower fees than other annuities, optional riders like lifetime income guarantees may carry additional costs. Understand these fees before committing.

3. **Surrender Periods:** Most FIAs have a surrender charge if you withdraw funds early. Make sure the surrender period aligns with your financial timeline.

4. **Insurance Carrier Reputation:** Work with a reputable insurer with strong financial ratings. This ensures your money is secure over the long term.

Consider consulting with a financial advisor who specializes in retirement planning to ensure you're selecting an FIA tailored to your needs and objectives.

Independent Ratings

Annuity ratings are **evaluations of an insurance company's financial strength and ability to meet its long-term obligations**, particularly when paying out annuity benefits. These ratings are provided by **major independent agencies**, including **AM Best, Standard & Poor's (S&P), Moody's, and Fitch**. Each agency uses its own rating scale to assess an insurer's ability to handle claims and remain solvent, with higher ratings (e.g., **A or A+**) indicating strong financial stability and lower ratings (e.g., **B or below**) signaling potential risk. When selecting an annuity, investors should prioritize insurers with **high ratings** to ensure the company can meet future income guarantees and contract obligations, especially for long-term retirement planning.

Ratings Flaws

While annuity ratings from agencies like **AM Best, Standard & Poor's (S&P), Moody's, and Fitch** provide valuable insights into an insurer's financial stability, the system has notable flaws. **First, ratings focus on the insurer's overall ability to pay claims, not on specific annuity products**, meaning a highly rated company could still offer less competitive annuities. **Second, rating agencies rely on the insurer's self-reported financial data**, which may not always reflect real-time risks, especially during economic downturns. **Third, rating agencies have conflicts of interest**, as insurers often pay for their own evaluations, potentially influencing ratings. Lastly, **ratings do not account for state guaranty associations**, which provide a safety net for policyholders in case of insurer insolvency, making ratings just one of many factors to consider when selecting an annuity provider.

Ratings Examples:

Ratings	
A.M. Best :	A++
Moody's:	A2
Standard & Poor's:	A+
Weiss:	NR

Ratings	
A.M. Best :	A+
Fitch:	A+
Moody's:	A1
Standard & Poor's:	A+

Ratings	
A.M. Best :	B++
Fitch:	A-
Standard & Poor's:	A-

Selecting Optimal Index Strategies

Once you've chosen the right FIA, the next step is selecting the optimal index strategies. FIAs typically allow you to allocate funds among various strategies that track different market indices. This flexibility enables you to customize your approach based on your risk tolerance and financial goals.

Common index strategies include:

- **Point-to-Point:** This measures the performance of an index over a set period, such as one year. It's straightforward and predictable, making it ideal for conservative investors.

- **Monthly Averaging:** This strategy calculates the index's average performance over a series of months. It's less volatile and can smooth out returns in choppy markets.

- **Participation Rates and Spreads:** Some strategies may involve a participation rate (the percentage of index growth you capture) or a spread (a deduction from the index's growth). Understand how these impact your returns.

The key is diversification. Rather than placing all your funds into one strategy, consider splitting allocations among multiple strategies to balance risk and reward. For example, you might allocate 50% to a point-to-point strategy and 50% to a monthly averaging strategy. This ensures you're not overly reliant on one approach and can capture growth in various market conditions.

Structuring the Conversion

Structuring your Roth conversion is where the planning becomes execution. The goal is to convert funds in a tax-efficient manner while staying within your desired tax bracket.

Here are the steps to structure your conversion effectively:

1. **Determine Your Conversion Amount:** Start by calculating how much of your traditional IRA or 401(k) you're willing to convert. Many retirees opt for partial conversions over several years to avoid being pushed into a higher tax bracket.

2. **Identify Low-Income Years:** Conversion is most advantageous in years when your income is lower, but not always. For example, if you've recently retired but haven't yet started Social Security or required minimum distributions, this may be an ideal time. Doing some conversions to reduce RMD's could still be a good strategy.

3. **Coordinate with Tax Brackets:** Use a tax calculator or consult with a CPA to ensure your conversion doesn't push you into an undesirably high tax bracket. Staying just below thresholds can help you avoid higher effective tax rates.

4. **Plan for Tax Payments:** Remember, taxes on conversions are due in the year of conversion. Ensure you have funds set aside to cover this liability, ideally from non-retirement accounts, so you don't deplete your retirement savings.

Marginal Tax Rate vs. Effective Tax Rate: Key Differences

1. What Is a Marginal Tax Rate?

The **marginal tax rate** is the tax percentage applied to **your last dollar of taxable income**. The U.S. has a **progressive tax system**, meaning different portions of your income fall into different **tax brackets**, each taxed at a different rate. Your **marginal tax rate** is the highest tax bracket you reach.

2. What Is an Effective Tax Rate?

The **effective tax rate** is the **average** tax rate you pay on your **total taxable income**. It is calculated as:

$$\text{Effective Tax Rate} = \frac{\text{Total Taxes Paid}}{\text{Total Taxable Income}}$$

Since only a **portion** of your income is taxed at each bracket's rate, your **effective tax rate is always lower than your marginal tax rate**.

Required Paperwork and Process

The administrative side of a Roth conversion may seem daunting, but it's relatively straightforward with proper guidance. Here's what you need to know about the paperwork and process:

1. **Contact Your Plan Administrator:** Start by reaching out to the financial institution managing your IRA or 401(k). They will provide the necessary forms for initiating a Roth conversion.

2. **Complete the Conversion Form:** This typically includes details such as the amount to convert, the account to transfer funds to, and your tax withholding preferences. Double-check all information to avoid delays.

3. **Open a Roth IRA Account:** If you don't already have one, you'll need to open a Roth IRA account to receive the converted funds.

4. **Confirm Tax Withholding:** Decide whether to have taxes withheld during the conversion or pay them separately. Many experts recommend paying taxes out of pocket to maximize the amount converted.

5. **Monitor the Transfer:** Once the paperwork is submitted, monitor the process to ensure funds are transferred correctly and in a timely manner. Keep all documentation for your records and future tax filings.

Common Implementation Pitfalls

Even with careful planning, there are common pitfalls to be aware of when implementing a Roth conversion strategy. By understanding these risks, you can take proactive steps to avoid them:

- **Underestimating Taxes:** One of the biggest mistakes retirees make is underestimating the tax impact of a conversion. Work closely with a CPA or financial advisor to calculate your tax liability accurately.

- **Triggering Higher Medicare Premiums:** Converting too much in a single year can increase your modified adjusted gross income (MAGI), which may result in higher Medicare premiums. Plan conversions to stay below key MAGI thresholds.

- **Market Timing Missteps:** Some retirees attempt to time the market before converting, but this approach can backfire. Focus on long-term benefits rather than short-term fluctuations.

- **Neglecting Estate Planning:** Roth conversions can have significant implications for your estate. Ensure your beneficiary designations are up to date and align with your overall legacy goals.

- **Failing to Diversify:** Don't put all your eggs in one basket. Diversify your retirement savings across multiple strategies, including Roth accounts, FIAs, and other investment vehicles.

By addressing these pitfalls head-on, you can ensure your Roth conversion strategy is executed smoothly and effectively, setting you up for a tax-efficient and secure retirement.

Chapter 6: Advanced Strategies

The FIA-Roth Conversion Strategy is not a one-size-fits-all approach. For retirees with more complex financial needs or higher retirement savings, advanced strategies can unlock additional benefits. This chapter delves into using multiple Fixed Indexed Annuities (FIAs), leveraging income riders, and exploring estate planning, asset protection, charitable giving, and legacy planning opportunities.

Using Multiple FIAs

Why Consider Multiple FIAs?

For retirees with significant retirement assets, using multiple FIAs can enhance flexibility, diversify risk, and optimize outcomes. Each FIA offers unique features, such as varying crediting methods, participation rates, or bonuses. By leveraging multiple products, you can:

- Diversify your portfolio to protect against market volatility.
- Match specific financial goals, such as income generation, growth, or legacy planning.
- Take advantage of different terms or conditions that align with your retirement timeline.

Case Study: Diversifying with Multiple FIAs

Scenario: Linda, 67, has $800,000 in her IRA and wants to convert to a Roth IRA while ensuring her assets grow tax-free. After consulting her retirement specialist, she divides her assets into three FIAs:

1. **FIA A**: Focused on growth with a high participation rate tied to the S&P 500.
2. **FIA B**: Includes a guaranteed income rider to cover essential living expenses.
3. **FIA C**: Provides a premium bonus and a shorter surrender period for flexibility.

Outcome: By using multiple FIAs, Linda balances growth potential, guaranteed income, and liquidity while optimizing her tax efficiency through strategic Roth conversions.

Leveraging Income Riders

What Are Income Riders?

Income riders are optional features that can be added to FIAs, providing guaranteed income for life. This feature can be especially useful during retirement to cover fixed expenses without relying on market-dependent withdrawals. Some key benefits include:

- **Guaranteed Lifetime Income**: Ensures you won't outlive your savings.
- **Flexibility**: Many riders allow for income deferral, increasing payouts the longer you wait.
- **Spousal Protection**: Some income riders provide joint benefits, ensuring both spouses receive income.

How to Maximize Income Riders in Roth Conversions

When combined with a Roth IRA, income riders can provide tax-free income for life. Here's how to make the most of them:

1. **Start Early**: Adding an income rider during the FIA's early years allows you to accumulate higher payout rates.

2. **Deferral Bonuses**: Choose income riders with deferral bonuses to maximize future income.

3. **Coordinate with Roth Conversions**: Convert assets to Roth IRAs first, then activate income riders to ensure payouts are tax-free.

Case Study: Guaranteed Income with Tax-Free Benefits

Scenario: Bob and Karen, both 62, are converting $400,000 to a Roth IRA over five years. They select an FIA with an income rider offering a 7% deferral bonus. By the time they activate the rider at age 70, their guaranteed income is $40,000 annually, entirely tax-free.

Outcome: Bob and Karen's Roth conversion strategy ensures they have a steady income stream without worrying about taxes or market volatility.

Estate Planning Benefits

How FIAs Enhance Estate Planning

Fixed Indexed Annuities can play a pivotal role in estate planning, ensuring your assets are passed on efficiently and tax-free. Key benefits include:

- **Avoiding Probate**: FIA death benefits pass directly to beneficiaries, bypassing probate.

- **Tax-Free Inheritance**: When combined with a Roth IRA, the death benefit becomes tax-free for heirs.
- **Flexibility**: Many FIAs offer payout options, allowing beneficiaries to choose a lump sum or lifetime income.

Strategies for Estate Planning

1. **Roth Conversion for Tax-Free Legacy**: Convert traditional retirement accounts to Roth IRAs and use FIAs to grow these assets. The death benefit will pass tax-free to heirs.
2. **Naming Multiple Beneficiaries**: Divide FIA benefits among children, grandchildren, or charities to distribute wealth efficiently.
3. **Spousal Continuation**: Choose spousal continuation options to ensure the surviving spouse retains benefits without interruption.

Are Annuity Death Benefits Tax-Free?

The tax treatment of annuity death benefits depends on how the annuity was funded, who the beneficiary is, and how the money is distributed. In most cases, annuity death benefits are not completely tax-free, but there are strategies to minimize taxes.

1. Annuities Inside a Roth IRA or Roth 401(k) → Tax-Free Death Benefit

- If the annuity was purchased with Roth IRA or Roth 401(k) funds, the death benefit is tax-free for beneficiaries, as long as the Roth account has been open for at least 5 years.

- Beneficiaries can withdraw the full death benefit tax-free or stretch withdrawals over time with no tax liability.

Best for tax-free inheritance.

2. Annuities Inside a Traditional IRA or 401(k) → Fully Taxable to Beneficiaries

- If the annuity was purchased inside a traditional IRA or 401(k), the entire death benefit is taxable as ordinary income when withdrawn.
- Beneficiaries must take Required Minimum Distributions (RMDs) based on IRS rules or withdraw the full balance within 10 years.

Full amount is subject to income tax at the beneficiary's tax rate.

3. Non-Qualified Annuities (Purchased with After-Tax Dollars) → Partially Taxable

- If the annuity was purchased outside of an IRA or 401(k) (i.e., with after-tax money), only the earnings (growth) are taxable—not the original premium paid.
- Beneficiaries can choose:
    - Lump Sum Payout → Immediate taxation on all gains.
    - Non-Qualified Stretch Option → Withdraw gradually and spread out the tax burden.

Principal is tax-free, but earnings are taxed as ordinary income.

4. Enhanced Death Benefit Riders → Taxable Unless in a Roth

- Some annuities include an enhanced death benefit rider that increases the payout amount.
- The additional benefit is taxed as ordinary income, unless the annuity is inside a Roth IRA.

Extra payout = extra taxes (unless Roth-funded).

5. How to Minimize Taxes on Annuity Death Benefits

- Fund the annuity with Roth IRA funds for tax-free inheritance.
- Spread withdrawals over multiple years to avoid a large tax hit in a single year.
- Use life insurance to pass wealth tax-free instead of annuities.
- Name a spouse as the beneficiary, as they can roll the annuity into their own IRA and delay taxes.

Case Study: Building a Tax-Free Legacy

Scenario: Susan, a 68-year-old widow, has $500,000 in her IRA. She converts it to a Roth IRA using an FIA with a 10% premium bonus. Upon her passing, her two children receive a tax-free inheritance of $550,000.

Outcome: Susan's proactive planning ensures her legacy is preserved and distributed tax-efficiently.

Asset Protection Features

Why Asset Protection Matters

For retirees, protecting assets from creditors, lawsuits, or unexpected financial events is critical. FIAs offer robust asset protection features, including:

- **Creditor Protection**: Many states protect annuities from creditors, ensuring your assets remain intact.
- **Guaranteed Minimum Value**: Even during market downturns, FIAs provide a guaranteed minimum value.
- **Liquidity Features**: Access funds during emergencies through penalty-free withdrawals for specific circumstances, such as terminal illness.

Case Study: Securing Assets from Unforeseen Risks
Scenario: John, 70, faces a potential lawsuit related to his former business. He's relieved to learn that his FIA assets are protected under state law, ensuring his retirement savings remain secure.
Outcome: John's choice to use FIAs not only provided retirement income but also safeguarded his wealth from legal risks.

Charitable Giving Strategies

Using FIAs for Charitable Contributions

FIAs can be an excellent vehicle for retirees looking to give back to their communities while optimizing tax benefits. Key strategies include:

1. **Qualified Charitable Distributions (QCDs)**: Although QCDs cannot be made directly from Roth IRAs, retirees can fund FIAs within traditional IRAs and direct QCDs to charities before converting.
2. **Designating Charities as Beneficiaries**: Name a charity as the beneficiary of your FIA or Roth IRA to leave a lasting impact.

3. **Charitable Gift Annuities**: Use part of your Roth conversion savings to fund charitable gift annuities, providing both a tax deduction and income.

Case Study: Leaving a Charitable Legacy
Scenario: Mary, 72, converts $300,000 to a Roth IRA and designates her alma mater as the beneficiary of her FIA death benefit. Upon her passing, the university receives a $350,000 tax-free gift.
Outcome: Mary's strategy supports a cause she loves while maximizing her tax efficiency.

Legacy Planning Opportunities
Combining FIAs with Roth Conversions for Legacy Planning
Legacy planning ensures your wealth benefits future generations. By combining FIAs and Roth conversions, retirees can:

- **Eliminate Taxes for Heirs**: Roth IRA assets grow tax-free, and distributions to beneficiaries are also tax-free.

- **Provide Lifetime Income**: FIAs with income riders can provide heirs with guaranteed income streams.

- **Simplify Wealth Transfer**: Annuity death benefits are distributed directly to beneficiaries, avoiding delays.

Advanced Legacy Strategies
1. **Generational Wealth Transfer**: Use Roth IRAs funded by FIAs to create multi-generational wealth that grows tax-free.

2. **Trust Integration**: Place FIAs within a trust to control the timing and distribution of assets to beneficiaries.

3. **Incentivized Inheritance**: Use annuity payout options to incentivize heirs, such as funding education or rewarding career milestones.

Case Study: Planning for Future Generations
Scenario: George, 65, uses a $1 million Roth IRA to fund two FIAs. He designates his three grandchildren as beneficiaries. The FIAs offer guaranteed income streams for each grandchild, ensuring financial security for decades.
Outcome: George's thoughtful planning creates a lasting legacy, helping his family thrive while avoiding taxes.

By implementing these advanced strategies, retirees can maximize the benefits of the FIA-Roth Conversion Strategy. From enhancing income security to leaving a tax-efficient legacy, these approaches ensure that your retirement plan adapts to your goals and values.

PART IV: ONGOING MANAGEMENT

Chapter 7: Monitoring and Adjusting

Annual Review Checklist

The success of a Roth conversion strategy hinges on consistent monitoring and periodic adjustments. Here's an annual review checklist to ensure your plan stays on track:

1. **Assess Your Tax Bracket**: Review your current and projected tax brackets. Work with a CPA to determine how much of your traditional retirement accounts you can convert to a Roth IRA without pushing yourself into a higher tax bracket. Understanding the marginal tax rates and thresholds for Medicare surcharges is crucial to avoid unexpected costs.

2. **Calculate the Optimal Conversion Amount**: Collaborate with your CPA and retirement specialist to calculate the optimal amount to convert each year. The goal is to maximize conversions during years with lower taxable income while keeping future tax liabilities in mind.

3. **Review Retirement Account Performance**: Evaluate the performance of your Fixed Indexed Annuities (FIAs) and other retirement accounts. Are your accounts meeting your growth expectations? This is essential to ensure you're converting at the right time.

4. **Analyze Changes in Personal Circumstances**: Have there been significant changes in your financial situation, health, or income? These changes can impact how much you should convert and when.

5. **Consider Legislative Updates**: Tax laws change. Ensure your CPA is up-to-date with the latest legislation that may impact Roth conversions, Required Minimum Distributions (RMDs), or FIA regulations.

6. **Revisit Estate Planning Goals**: If you aim to leave a tax-free inheritance, evaluate how your current Roth conversion strategy aligns with your legacy objectives. Confirm that beneficiary designations on FIAs and Roth IRAs are accurate.

Market Condition Considerations

Market fluctuations and interest rate changes play a significant role in determining the timing and amount of Roth conversions. Here's what to consider:

1. **Market Downturns**: A market downturn presents an opportunity to convert traditional retirement account assets while their value is temporarily lower. This reduces the taxable income triggered by the conversion and allows future growth to occur in the tax-free environment of a Roth IRA.

2. **Market Volatility**: FIAs offer protection against market losses while providing market-linked gains. If the broader market experiences significant volatility, re-evaluate the timing of conversions to minimize risk and maximize returns.

3. **Interest Rate Environment**: Rising interest rates can impact the returns of Fixed Indexed Annuities. Monitor interest rate trends and consider how they affect the growth potential of your FIAs and overall retirement strategy.

4. **Tax Rate Predictions**: Consult with your advisor about anticipated changes to federal and state tax rates. If tax rates are expected to increase, it may be wise to accelerate conversions.

When to Accelerate or Pause Conversions
Roth conversions are not a "set it and forget it" strategy. Here's when to accelerate or pause conversions:
Accelerate Conversions:

- **Tax Rates Are Low**: Take advantage of historically low tax rates before they increase.

- **Market Corrections**: Convert during a market correction to capitalize on lower account values.

- **Life Events**: If you've experienced a significant drop in income (e.g., early retirement or business sale), consider accelerating conversions to maximize the lower tax bracket.

- **Anticipated Tax Law Changes**: Speed up conversions if there's a credible risk of rising taxes or policy changes affecting retirement accounts.

Pause Conversions:

- **Entering a Higher Tax Bracket**: Avoid pushing yourself into a higher tax bracket unless absolutely necessary.

- **Unexpected Income Increases**: Postpone conversions if you've had a one-time income spike, such as a large capital gain.
- **Health Changes**: If significant medical expenses are anticipated, you might qualify for itemized deductions that reduce taxable income, potentially allowing for larger conversions later.

Rebalancing Strategies

Rebalancing your portfolio is a critical part of ongoing management. Here's how to approach it:

1. **Rebalance After a Conversion**: After converting funds to a Roth IRA, reassess your asset allocation. Consider allocating more growth-oriented assets to the Roth IRA since its gains will be tax-free. This is especially effective if you have a Guaranteed Income Annuity in place already that covers your base monthly expenses.
2. **Maintain FIA Allocation**: Ensure your FIAs are performing as expected. If one annuity underperforms or if better products become available, consider reallocating funds.
3. **Diversify Across Tax Buckets**: Aim to maintain a balance between taxable, tax-deferred, and tax-free accounts to give yourself flexibility in managing taxes and income during retirement.
4. **Adjust for Market Performance**: Use market gains to rebalance without incurring additional taxes. For example, shift growth from taxable accounts into your Roth IRA.

5. **Review Risk Tolerance**: As you age, your risk tolerance may decrease. Periodically review your risk exposure and adjust accordingly.

Exit Strategies if Needed

While Roth conversions can be a powerful strategy, circumstances may arise where you need to pause or modify your plan. Here are potential exit strategies:

1. **Partial Conversions**: If taxes or personal circumstances make full conversions impractical, consider partial conversions over an extended period.

2. **Recharacterization (If Available)**: Although recent tax law changes eliminated recharacterizations for Roth conversions, stay informed about potential future legislative changes that might reinstate this option.

3. **FIA Liquidity Options**: Leverage the liquidity features of your Fixed Indexed Annuities to meet unexpected expenses or reduce conversion amounts temporarily.

4. **Tax-Exempt Investments**: Shift focus to other tax-exempt investments like municipal bonds if your conversion strategy needs to be paused.

5. **Legacy Adjustments**: If your priorities shift toward estate planning, reassess how much you want to leave in tax-deferred accounts versus converting to Roth IRAs for tax-free inheritance.

By staying proactive with these monitoring and adjustment strategies, retirees can maximize the benefits of the FIA-Roth Conversion Strategy. Regular reviews and adaptations ensure that your financial plan evolves alongside market conditions, tax laws, and personal circumstances, ultimately securing a more predictable and tax-efficient retirement.

Chapter 8: Special Situations

Business Owner Considerations

For business owners, the opportunity to leverage Roth conversions is often unique and requires careful consideration of both short-term and long-term tax strategies. As a business owner, you may have access to multiple retirement plans, such as SEP IRAs, SIMPLE IRAs, or even solo 401(k)s. These plans offer valuable benefits, but they also come with potential tax liabilities in retirement. Let's break down the key considerations:

1. **Tax Timing and Cash Flow Management** Converting traditional retirement accounts to a Roth IRA creates an immediate tax liability, which can significantly impact your business's cash flow. Timing is everything. If your business is experiencing a low-income year due to market fluctuations or other factors, this might be the perfect time to initiate a Roth conversion. This strategy allows you to minimize the effective tax rate on the conversion while securing future tax-free growth.

2. **Sale of a Business** If you're planning to sell your business, the proceeds can trigger a significant tax event. However, strategic Roth conversions before the sale can reduce your overall tax burden. By converting portions of your retirement accounts

incrementally in the years leading up to the sale, you can avoid being pushed into the highest tax brackets.

3. **Succession Planning**
   A Roth conversion can also play a critical role in business succession planning. If you plan to pass your business to your heirs, converting to a Roth IRA can ensure that they inherit a tax-free account, allowing for smoother financial transitions.

Hypothetical Case Study:
Sarah owns a small marketing agency and expects to sell her business within five years. She consults a financial advisor and begins annual Roth conversions during low-income years. By the time she sells her business, her tax liability is significantly reduced, and her retirement accounts are entirely Roth, securing tax-free income for her retirement years.

Real Estate Investors
Real estate investors face unique challenges and opportunities when it comes to Roth conversions. Real estate often generates passive income, and the depreciation benefits can offset that income, creating strategic windows for tax planning.

1. **Leveraging Depreciation**
   Real estate investors can use depreciation to their advantage during Roth conversions. By offsetting rental income with depreciation, you might find yourself in a lower effective tax bracket, making a Roth conversion more affordable.

2. **Equity and Roth Conversions**
   Many real estate investors have significant equity in

their properties. A 1031 exchange can help defer taxes on property sales, but combining this strategy with Roth conversions offers long-term tax benefits. For example, during a year when you sell a property, consider converting a portion of your retirement accounts to take advantage of lower effective tax rates.

3. **Passive Loss Carryforward** If you've accumulated passive loss carryforward, you may be able to offset the taxable income from a Roth conversion, further reducing the tax burden.

Hypothetical Case Study:
James owns several rental properties and takes advantage of depreciation to offset his taxable income. In a year when one property has high maintenance costs, he performs a partial Roth conversion, leveraging his lower tax bracket and securing future tax-free growth.

High Net Worth Strategies
High net worth individuals, generally defined as those with $1 million or more in investable assets, face a different set of challenges when considering Roth conversions due to the complexity of their financial situations. These complexities include the impact on estate taxes, potential increases in Medicare premiums, and the need for integrated tax and legacy planning. However, these challenges can be mitigated with proper planning and strategic coordination of resources.

1. **Avoiding Medicare Surcharges** For high earners, Roth conversions can trigger higher Medicare premiums due to increased Modified Adjusted Gross Income (MAGI). To

minimize this impact, consider spreading conversions over multiple years to stay below the Medicare Income-Related Monthly Adjustment Amount (IRMAA) thresholds.

2. **Legacy Planning**
   A Roth IRA is a powerful tool for legacy planning. High net worth individuals can use Roth conversions to reduce the taxable income their heirs might face. Additionally, Roth IRAs are not subject to Required Minimum Distributions (RMDs), allowing the account to grow tax-free for decades.

3. **Charitable Giving**
   Pairing Roth conversions with charitable contributions can be a win-win. High net worth individuals can use a Donor-Advised Fund (DAF) to offset the tax liability of a Roth conversion, maximizing both philanthropic impact and retirement savings.

Hypothetical Case Study:
Patricia, a retiree with $5 million in retirement accounts, starts annual Roth conversions while making large charitable donations through her DAF. She keeps her taxable income manageable, reduces future RMDs, and secures a tax-free inheritance for her children.

Early Retirement Planning
If you're planning to retire early, Roth conversions can be a cornerstone of your strategy. Early retirees often have several years of low taxable income before Social Security and RMDs begin, creating a prime window for conversions.

1. **Bridging the Gap**
   Roth conversions can provide tax-free income during the gap years between early retirement and the start of Social Security. By converting funds while in a lower tax bracket, you're setting yourself up for long-term success.

2. **Tax Diversification**
   Early retirees benefit from tax diversification—the ability to draw from taxable, tax-deferred, and tax-free accounts. This strategy reduces the risk of high taxes in later years.

Hypothetical Case Study:
Karen retires at 55 with $800,000 in her IRA. Over the next 10 years, she converts her IRA to a Roth IRA, staying in a low tax bracket. By age 65, she has a fully tax-free account to supplement her Social Security benefits.

Healthcare Cost Planning
Healthcare costs are a significant concern in retirement, and Roth conversions can help address this issue in several ways.

1. **Avoiding Tax Bracket Creep**
   Future healthcare costs, including long-term care, can push retirees into higher tax brackets. Roth conversions help mitigate this risk by reducing taxable income in retirement.

2. **Medicare Premium Planning**
   By managing the timing and size of Roth conversions, you can avoid crossing IRMAA thresholds, keeping your Medicare premiums lower.

3. **Tax-Free Withdrawals for Healthcare Costs** Withdrawals from a Roth IRA are tax-free, making them an ideal source of funds for unexpected medical expenses.

Hypothetical Case Study:
John, age 62, anticipates high healthcare costs in his later years. He starts Roth conversions early, keeping his MAGI below IRMAA thresholds. By the time he turns 70, his Roth IRA provides a tax-free buffer for medical expenses.

Working with Professional Advisors

Roth conversions are complex, and working with a team of professional advisors can ensure you're making the best decisions for your financial future.

1. **Retirement Specialists** Retirement specialists focus on decumulating assets during the critical years 5 years before and after retirement. They can help create a personalized strategy that optimizes Roth conversions while ensuring sustainable income.

2. **Tax Advisors and CPAs** A Certified Public Accountant (CPA) or tax advisor can identify opportunities to minimize the tax impact of Roth conversions, such as timing conversions during low-income years or leveraging deductions.

3. **Estate Planning Attorneys** An estate planning attorney can help you align Roth conversions with your legacy goals, ensuring a smooth transfer of wealth to your heirs.

Hypothetical Case Study:

David consults a retirement specialist, CPA, and estate attorney to coordinate his Roth conversion strategy. Together, they create a plan that minimizes taxes, avoids Medicare surcharges, and secures a tax-free inheritance for his grandchildren.

Glossary of Terms

1. **Backdoor Roth IRA**: A strategy allowing high-income earners to fund a Roth IRA through conversions.
2. **Beneficiary Bonus**: A feature in some FIAs that provides an enhanced death benefit for heirs.
3. **Caps**: The maximum interest rate an annuity can earn during a set period, limiting growth potential but ensuring stability.
4. **Charitable Gift Annuity**: A strategy allowing retirees to fund a charity while receiving tax benefits and income.
5. **Charitable Giving**: Using retirement accounts to make tax-efficient donations to charities.
6. **Deferred Income**: Income that is delayed to a future date, often growing with interest or bonuses in FIAs.
7. **Estate Planning**: Preparing to transfer assets tax-efficiently to heirs or beneficiaries.
8. **Estate Tax Exemption**: The amount of wealth that can be transferred to heirs tax-free under federal or state laws.

9. **Five-Year Rule**: A Roth IRA regulation requiring converted funds to stay in the account for at least five years to avoid penalties on withdrawals.

10. **Fixed Indexed Annuity (FIA)**: A retirement product that offers market-indexed growth potential while protecting the principal from losses.

11. **Guaranteed Lifetime Withdrawal Benefit (GLWB)**: An FIA rider that provides a fixed annual income for life.

12. **Income Rider**: An optional feature in annuities guaranteeing a steady income stream for life.

13. **Income-Related Monthly Adjustment Amount (IRMAA)**: Higher Medicare premiums for individuals with higher taxable incomes.

14. **Index Crediting Strategy**: The method used to calculate interest earned based on market index performance.

15. **Legacy Planning**: Strategies to preserve and transfer wealth, often tax-free, to future generations using tools like Roth IRAs and FIAs.

16. **Liquidity**: The availability of funds for withdrawal without significant penalties, especially important in annuities with surrender charges.

17. **MAGI (Modified Adjusted Gross Income)**: An adjusted income figure used to determine eligibility for Roth contributions and Medicare premiums.

18. **Market Volatility**: Fluctuations in market prices that can affect retirement investments; FIAs protect against these risks.

19. **Multi-Year Conversion**: A Roth conversion strategy that spreads tax liabilities over several years to minimize tax bracket increases.

20. **Participation Rate**: The percentage of market index growth credited to an annuity.

21. **Point-to-Point Crediting**: An FIA strategy that calculates returns based on the change in an index's value between two specific dates.

22. **Premium Bonus**: An upfront bonus offered by FIAs to boost initial investments.

23. **Probate**: A legal process to distribute a deceased person's estate, which can be avoided with proper estate planning tools like FIAs.

24. **Pro-Rata Rule**: IRS rule requiring proportional taxation of pre-tax and after-tax funds during a conversion.

25. **Required Minimum Distributions (RMDs)**: Mandatory withdrawals from traditional retirement accounts starting at age 73.

26. **Roth Conversion**: The process of transferring funds from a traditional IRA or 401(k) to a Roth IRA, paying taxes upfront for tax-free growth and withdrawals in retirement.

27. **Sequence of Returns Risk**: The risk of receiving lower or negative returns early in retirement, which can impact long-term savings sustainability.

28. **Social Security Taxation**: Taxation of Social Security benefits based on combined income, which can be impacted by Roth conversions.

29. **Spousal Continuation**: A provision in annuities allowing a surviving spouse to continue receiving benefits without disruption.

30. **Spread**: A fixed deduction from the market's growth before crediting to an annuity.

31. **Tax Bracket**: A range of incomes taxed at a specific rate.

32. **Tax Cuts and Jobs Act (TCJA)**: Legislation that reduced tax rates and expanded brackets, influencing Roth conversion strategies.

33. **Tax-Free Growth**: Investment gains in a Roth IRA that are not subject to taxes.

34. **Tax-Free Inheritance**: Assets passed to heirs through Roth IRAs or FIAs without tax obligations.

35. **Taxable Income**: Income subject to taxation, including Roth conversions that are treated as ordinary income for the conversion year.

For Additional Support:

We are here to help. Request your free Social Security Analysis and retirement Income Plan. If you would like personalized guidance in maximizing your Social Security benefits and creating a comprehensive retirement income strategy, please contact:

Boom Retirement Solutions
(888) 839-1611

SCAN TO SCHEDULE

AN APPOINTMENT

For a free copy of our other book "Maximizing Social Security Benefits" send an email to jeff@boomretirement.com and in the Subject Line write "Free Book Social Security."

Made in the USA
Monee, IL
13 September 2026

62981858R00069